I'm so sick of books of people telling us what we need to do and how to walk but have never walked through it themselves. These messages ring hollow to a generation that is looking for fathers and mothers who have walked through real things in their life and who have come through on the other side to feed a generation with a living understanding of who God is and how God delivered them from fear. Thank God for Jeremy Johnson and his new book, *Declare War on Fear,* because this book didn't come from a good Bible study but from the dark night where Jeremy discovered the God who breaks the spirit of fear.

God has raised up Jeremy and his wife Christy for such a time as this to deliver a generation marked by anxiety, fear, and depression. I wholeheartedly endorse this book and even more its author.

COREY RUSSELL
Author of *Teach Us to Pray*

In his book, *Declare War on Fear,* my friend Pastor Jeremy Johnson does not shame us for our fear but validates our feelings and teaches us how to persevere in our calling despite them. When we stop letting our feelings dictate our destination and walk in step with the spirit of power and love, we are sanctified and God is glorified.

SAMUEL RODRIGUEZ
New Season Church Lead Pastor
NHCLC President/CEO
Author, *Persevere With Power; What Heaven Starts,
Hell Cannot Stop!*
Exec. Producer, *Breakthrough* and *Flamin Hot'* movies

Jeremy is not only a powerhouse communicator but a personal friend. He has a prophetic voice for this generation, and his passion and enthusiasm to see revival on planet earth comes through in this book. This is not a self-help book; this is about conquering your fear before it conquers you. It's time to declare a war on fear!

MARTIN SANTIAGO
Social Club Misfits

This book was birthed in the fire. What you will read in these pages is not theory or opinion, but a message that has been formed on the front lines of battle. All of us face fear in some way, but the Bible is clear that we are not to give in to fear. Fear will steal your future and rob you of all that God has for you. The good news is that Jesus has given you the power to overcome fear. *Declare War on Fear* is the book we need in this generation. This message will inspire, encourage, and challenge you in the best of ways.

BANNING LIEBSCHER
Founder & Pastor of Jesus Culture

The enemy's most relentless and devastating weapon against God's own is the bombardment of lies that undermine our faith and cause us to question the character of God and our relationship with Him. The result is crippling, destiny-stealing FEAR. It began in the Garden with devastating consequences. Our only effective defence is a sound knowledge of God's Word and daily encounters with His Presence. Pastor Jeremy has unwrapped these so powerfully in his book, *Declare War on Fear*, and I thoroughly recommend it for every person who desires to walk "fearlessly" in their God-given purpose!

PASTOR RUSSELL EVANS
Senior Pastor, Planetshakers

Jeremy uses the pages of this book to examine not only the root of what causes so many of us to give up on the future God wants for us, but also as a practical guide to defuse our fears through the power of God. Lives will be changed by the insights he offers through his life and Scripture.

TAUREN WELLS
Celebrated recording artist, Songwriter

If there's anyone to motivate and teach you how to overcome fear in your life, it's Jeremy. I've attended his church, Fearless Church, in Los Angeles for the past couple years, and it's been the best church experience of my 12 year walk with Christ. I've come to know that a few of Jeremy's many strengths are that he has an incredible ability to encourage people, teach them, and empower them to overcome all types of obstacles in their life through Christ. After reading about his past in this book, his struggle with fear and how he gave things to God, I'm more encouraged to be available and to walk in courage.

GRAYSON BOUCHER (The Professor)
Actor, streetball legend

DECLARE WAR ON
FEAR

DETHRONE THE SPIRIT OF FEAR THAT WARS AGAINST YOUR DESTINY

JEREMY JOHNSON

DEDICATION

I want to dedicate this book to my beautiful wife who has helped me through so many fears. She is constantly reminding me that God is for me and not against me. She has helped me see the gift that is in me to give to others. She hasn't let me quit when I've tried time and time again and has contended for freedom time and time again. Thank you for your wisdom patience and love.

To my kids who also have fought for my freedom and reminded me time and time again to laugh, to have fun, and to trust God. To my daughter Lyric—for all the songs you've sang for me and prayers you prayed over me. To my son Brave—for your soft heart, always caring if Dad's all right when I've been down. To my little angel, Arrow, who makes me laugh and always asks for another snuggle.

To my Mom and Dad, who until this day fight for my freedom, and send me scriptures and encouraging prayers. To my amazing in-laws, Glen and Debbie, who have prayed and encouraged me to rise up to greatness.

To my savior Jesus Christ who has lifted me up and given me grace, and has called me to rule with him. To be fearless because of him.

DESTINY IMAGE® PUBLISHERS, INC.

P.O. Box 310, Shippensburg, PA 17257-0310

"Promoting Inspired Lives."

This book and all other Destiny Image and Destiny Image Fiction books are available at Christian bookstores and distributors worldwide.

For more information on foreign distributors, call 717-532-3040.

Reach us on the Internet: www.destinyimage.com.

ISBN 13 TP: 978-0-7684-6434-4

ISBN 13 eBook: 978-0-7684-6435-1

ISBN 13 HC: 978-0-7684-6437-5

ISBN 13 LP: 978-0-7684-6436-8

For Worldwide Distribution, Printed in the U.S.A.

1 2 3 4 5 6 7 8 / 27 26 25 24 23

CONTENT

FOREWORD

Fear is not a bullet, but a nuclear bomb that paralyzes every area of a person's life. This fear can linger for years or even a lifetime. Fear has an eternal engine that never shuts off in your mind. Fear does not have an off switch; it affects your decisions and your behavior. Fear thinks it has the last word, not God!

Jeremy Johnson has struggled, fought, and confronted the spirit of fear for years. God allowed him the ability to learn strategy in dealing with this demonic stronghold. He has confronted fear head-on, and his desire is to eradicate fear from people's lives. This book, *Declare War on Fear: Dethroning the Spirit that Wars Against Your Destiny*, will take you on a journey to freedom. Remember as you're reading that you will never overcome what you won't confront.

Everyone has something they're battling. You will face many losses in your life, but never let yourself be defeated. I have learned more about God through my pain, setbacks, and shattered dreams. I saw God's power and ability to carry me, to love me at my weakest, and give me the strength to conquer my fears. Through all these trials I've learned exactly what Jeremy wants his readers to learn—to love more and fear less. God loves us so much and everything we walk through in life can be used to help others walk through to victory.

We are never in control of what happens around us, but we are in control of what happens inside of us. Let Jeremy guide you to breakthrough and freedom from fear. As you travel through the pages of this book, you will encounter a young man battling for direction and affirmation. He shares his journey as a fearful young man who said yes to God and has become a fearless leader.

Jeremy is my son-in-law, married to my middle daughter Christy. God called them to plant a church in Los Angeles, to take territory for the Kingdom of God. They are anointed preachers and have had their share of setbacks. These setbacks did not stop them from their calling. They left behind the spirit of fear to love people relentlessly. Fear could've stopped them from saying yes to God, but instead they pursued God's perfect love that casts out fear.

As you read this book, remember that you have the power to say, "Fear is not how my story is going to end." These pages will teach you how to breathe peacefully again. They will challenge you to move forward. They will affirm to you that God has a great calling for your life. Remember, your desire to break free must be greater than your fear of failure. Let every story and every chapter give you the courage to love more and fear less!

GLEN BERTEAU
Glen Berteau Ministries, Colleyville, Texas
Author of *Why Am I Not Healed When God Promised, Christianity Lite* and *Christianity To-Go*

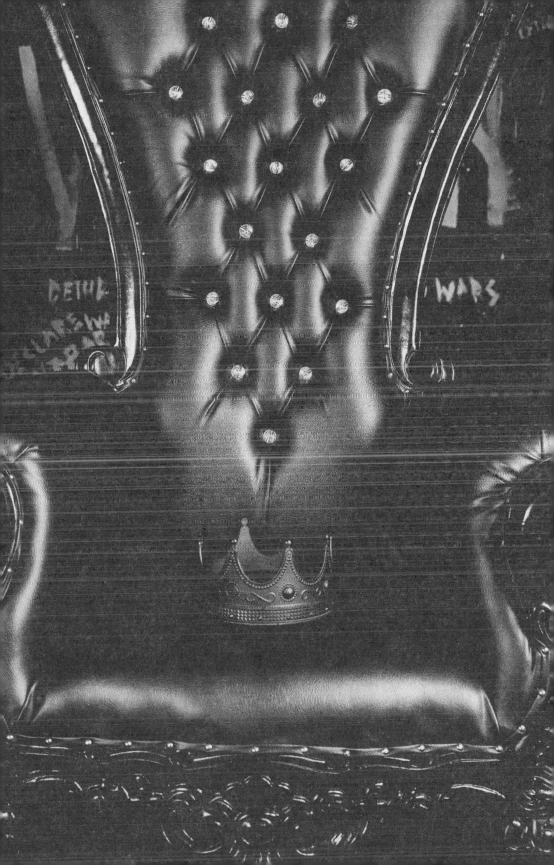

FEAR
WAGES WAR

CHAPTER

1

Fear is loud; it's brash. It works overtime to bring silence to its foes. It tells lies such as, "You will never [fill in the blank]." "You can't [fill it the blank.]" "You're never going to be [fill in the blank]." You have heard its taunts. Fear wages war in your head; the mind is the battleground. Fear is the believers' greatest foe, and it will do whatever it can to silence us and keep us bound. For all the things fear wants to lie to us about, God says to His Church, "Fear not!" To that paralyzing fear... not! "Fear, you're not going to win! We are not going to give you power; we are not going to live in your lies one more day. We're not going to bow or run. Today we will agree with God and proclaim, "Fear not!" over ourselves.

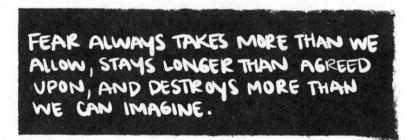

FEAR ALWAYS TAKES MORE THAN WE ALLOW, STAYS LONGER THAN AGREED UPON, AND DESTROYS MORE THAN WE CAN IMAGINE.

"Fear not!"—with two words, God draws a red line on fear's attack and simultaneously declares war on fear. It's time the sons and daughters of God do the same. The most dangerous place we can be as believers is in denial, thinking that if we just leave our fear alone it will go away. We buy the lie directly from fear's lips. How's that going for you? It's naive for us to think that fear left unchecked will leave us alone. We think that if we just avoid certain actions, circumstances, or people, we will keep fear at bay. However, fear always takes more than we allow, stays longer than agreed upon, and destroys more than we can imagine. Fear is so afraid of you becoming all that God designed you to be that it hunts you from a young age.

From personal experience, I have learned that fear never has its fill. It is always hungry for more…more of your dreams, more of your hopes, and more of your future. Fear never shrinks, it always grows. Give it an inch, it will take a mile. This is why we must choose today to declare war on fear. This declaration will only be successful with the right focus and the right fear. Yes, you read that right: you fight fear with fear. The Bible says in Proverbs 9:10, "The fear of the Lord is the beginning of wisdom." This is because it's not bad to fear; it's in whom you place your fear that brings life or death. Fear is just another word for reverence. This is why when we fear the Lord, we fear nothing else. When we give Him our reverence, we realize how big He is. He becomes not just Savior but Lord. When we give reverence to fear, we are by default removing God from the throne of our hearts. God, in His love, gives you the choice of choosing your king.

> *Now fear the LORD and serve him with all faithfulness. Throw away the gods your forefathers worshiped beyond the River and in Egypt, and serve the LORD. But if serving the LORD seems undesirable to you, then choose for yourselves this day whom you will serve, whether the gods your forefathers served beyond the River, or the gods of the Amorites, in whose land you are living. But as for me and my household, we will serve the LORD [Joshua 24:14–15 NIV].*

Your worry and your worship, both enthrone a spirit. For far too long, I allowed fear to live on that throne. I gave it permission to reign, whether it was paralyzing terrors at night or threats of

THE FEAR OF THE LORD IS A FOUNTAIN OF LIFE, SO THAT ONE MAY AVOID THE SNARES OF DEATH.

PROVERBS 14:27

the day. Don't buy into the lie that, "if you just ignore it, it will eventually go away. You can't drink it away; you can't counsel it away; you can't ignore it away. You must confront fear head-on. You must defeat fear. This is because fear is not an emotion or a feeling; at its core, it's a spirit, "For God has not given us a spirit of fear and timidity, but of power, love, and self-discipline" (2 Tim. 1:7 NLT). If fear is a spirit and not just a feeling, we must take aim and declare an all-out war. Fear comes to ravage your life. Today everything can change based on your declaration.

I had a friend that was always declaring and decreeing every time he prayed, and I asked him, "Why do you do that in your prayers?" He said because kings don't beg, they declare and they decree. Revelation 17:14 says, "He is Lord of lords and King of kings." So, if He's our King, then we must be kings and act kingly. That means, you have authority. God has called you to rule over things as a king. Many times we're waiting on God, but could it be that God is waiting on you? Could it be that you've been trying to live at peace with fear and ruining your peace with God? You may be saying to yourself, "This just runs in my family. This is the way it will always be; everyone has fears. This is the thorn in my flesh." Stop, and listen to yourself speak; you would never give this advice to someone else! When you believe this, that's when depression comes; that's when anxiety comes. When there is no light at the end of the tunnel, there is no hope. I have found fear never comes alone; it always brings its friends. Take your power back today. God gave you authority through the blood of Jesus, His death, burial, and resurrection. Today I challenge you to command this demonic spirit of fear to leave your life. When we enthrone Christ, we dethrone the spirit of fear. Fear only has power when you begin to believe its lies. Easy then, right? Simply don't believe its lies. But, we all know that it's not always that easy. The problem is that fear speaks lies mixed with truth. We call them half-truths, and a half-truth is a whole lie. When truth and lies mix, it's hard to separate fact from fiction. This is how fear plants itself in our hearts. The trick is that the lie masquerades as truth.

We've heard fear described as "False Evidence Appearing Real." Our fears manipulate the truth. This only wounds us when we believe the false evidence and allow it into the courtroom of our lives. As judge and jury we rule on the evidence presented and live defeated and locked away by fear. My prayer is that this book points you back to the truth, not just your truth. If you will choose to read this with an open mind and heart, I believe your battle with fear will end here. If He did it for me, He can do it for you. Let me show you how to love more and fear less. Notice the word picture in *fearless*; the main goal should be to take one more step toward love today, which is one step away from fear. As you do that, love actually kicks fear out of the rooms of your life. I want to take you on a journey in this book not of chasing down fear and taking it out, but of chasing down love and letting love take fear out. In 1 John 4:18, we see this truth, "Perfect love casts out fear" (NKJV). So, walk toward love with your eyes fixed, and watch as fear is expelled, and its charge on you is kicked out of the courtroom of your life. Perfect love is waiting to remove all your fear. Take the journey toward His throne of grace and pursue a fearless life today!

SET
APART

CHAPTER 2

Why is fear so consumed with you? Some would call

its behavior obsessed. It seems to have chosen you from a very young age to destroy your life—every dream, every relationship, every hope. You need to know fear did not choose you at random, and fear ignored never leaves. If fear is after you, it's because it sees more in you than you see in yourself. Fear pursues you to make you run from who you were destined to be. If you break fear's chains, it's in trouble. There is no greater threat to fear than a person fully free from its lies. No greater victory over fear than to be fully embracing your call. You have been chosen by God Himself for great things, and fear knows it. There is nothing it will stop at to see you held captive. However, just as fear is committed to your bondage, God is committed to His call on your life. That begins with freedom from fear!

> *Before I formed you in the womb I knew you, before you were born I set you apart; I appointed you as a prophet to the nations* (Jeremiah 1:5).

The call on your life, like a magnet to metal, is always pulling you toward it. You were set apart by God Himself.

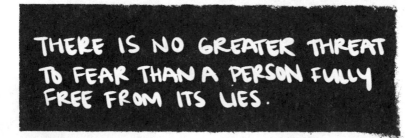

THERE IS NO GREATER THREAT TO FEAR THAN A PERSON FULLY FREE FROM ITS LIES.

STANDING OUT

I had no chance at fitting in. I was meant to stand out. Growing up, we lived in Galt, California, which stood for Great American

Little Town. It was a town of about 25,000 people and 100,000 cows. I grew up in a place where we would shoot guns in our backyards; it was normal, and no cops would be called. My trouble fitting in all began in third grade when I got a perm. Yes, I said it—a perm. My mom was a beautician in training, going to beauty school, and for homework she had to try the different things she was learning. She often brought home plastic heads with synthetic hair for practice, but when perms came in style, the synthetic hair would not do. She needed a guinea pig, a test rat. My dad had a real job so there was no way testing could be done on him. Who was next in line? Me, of course. I was too young to say no—how unfair! After seven hours, I had a perm. Perms are not just one-dimensional either, they affect every part of your life. They're scratch 'n' sniff, 3D, and they have a distinct smell; it was not a pleasing aroma to God or to anyone else, I'll tell you that. This perm made a young man who longed to stay hidden instantly stand out. I was a target for rejection and bullying; I got really good at fighting that year. After my first fight at school because I was being called names, I stormed home to my mom. "You did this to me! A perm, Mom? Are you kidding me?" Immediately she responded, "Don't worry, son. They are just jealous! You look like David Hasselhoff on Baywatch." And of course that helped because every kid wants to look like David Hasselhoff (not!).

THOSE WHO FIT IN, DON'T SEEK.

I wish I could say it got better when the perm went away, but it wasn't the case. I realize now it was never the perm, because for my whole life I have stood out. Standing out as an adult is different than standing out as a kid, though. As adults, a lot of us want to stand out from the crowd; we want to be different and unique. It's almost an achievement as an adult. However, this is not the case when you're younger, and by the time you reach adulthood, the damage has already been done to your self-esteem. Looking back after walking through healing, I can see that I never had a chance of fitting in because it was God Himself causing me to stand out. It was never the perm. It was nothing I was doing or not doing; it was God's greater purpose.

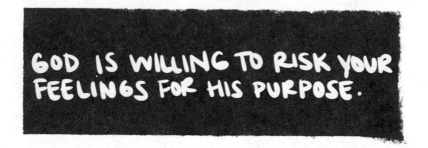

GOD IS WILLING TO RISK YOUR FEELINGS FOR HIS PURPOSE.

Those who fit in, don't seek. What I mean is that if at any point in time I would've fit into what was around me, I would've stopped searching for something deeper. It is that very search that led me to discover that He alone wanted to be my hope, my joy, and my peace. It was Him alone who was calling me. If I would've fit in with the crowd, I would've missed my call. I had to be alone to push me to Him.

For Moses, David, and many of the heroes of faith, the isolation and the awkwardness in their own skin led them to find something greater than themselves. Not fitting in sometimes makes you feel unseen, and that may be true. You might be unseen by man, but that doesn't mean you are unseen by God. At times, that lack of connection with man can make you feel like you have no value, so you morph into something else that you believe is desired. Their affirmation will never fulfill the loneliness inside your heart, though. God is willing to risk your feelings for His purpose. If you'll press into this purpose, you'll discover that it was God who set you apart so that you'd seek Him instead of them, the world's acceptance. It is only in God that you will find your true calling and identity.

> YOU ONLY HIDE WHAT IS VALUABLE, NOT BECAUSE YOU DON'T HAVE PURPOSE FOR IT, BUT BECAUSE THE PURPOSE IS NOT FOR EVERYDAY USE.

HIDDEN MOMENTS

In the Bible when God chose a man or woman for a job, we see a pattern of them being hidden before they are seen. God found Moses as a leader hidden in the desert, not in the palace. He found David hidden in a field, not a castle. He found Samson hidden in prison, not in a place of prestige. Lazarus was hidden in death, not life. Peter was hidden in his father's fishing business, not preaching. Paul was hidden in religion, not revival. Don't fear the hidden moments.

Maybe you're reading this book right now and feel hidden from man, or feeling as though God has forgotten you yet He remembers everyone else. Don't despise the times of being hidden, for it was the cave that prepared David to rule in the palace. It's the sheep Moses led that prepared him for the people of Israel. In the secret place, God is forging what will be seen one day. You only hide what is valuable, not because you don't have purpose for it, but because the purpose is not for everyday use. It's for moments of greatness. Jesus spent a lifetime being hidden to prepare Him for three years of ministry that would impact all of humanity. We pick the wrong man for the job most of the time; I've chosen the most qualified and the most talented. But God doesn't look at the outward things; He looks at the heart. God does not pick the qualified; He qualifies the called. God flexes when your strength is gone. God begins at impossible, because what is impossible for man is possible for God. When you are weak, He is strong. If I want to see God flex in my life, then I have to be okay with feeling unseen. I have to be okay with my weakness.

THE LORD IS MY LIGHT AND MY SALVATION; WHOM SHALL I FEAR? THE LORD IS THE STRONGHOLD OF MY LIFE; OF WHOM SHALL I BE AFRAID?

PSALM 27:1

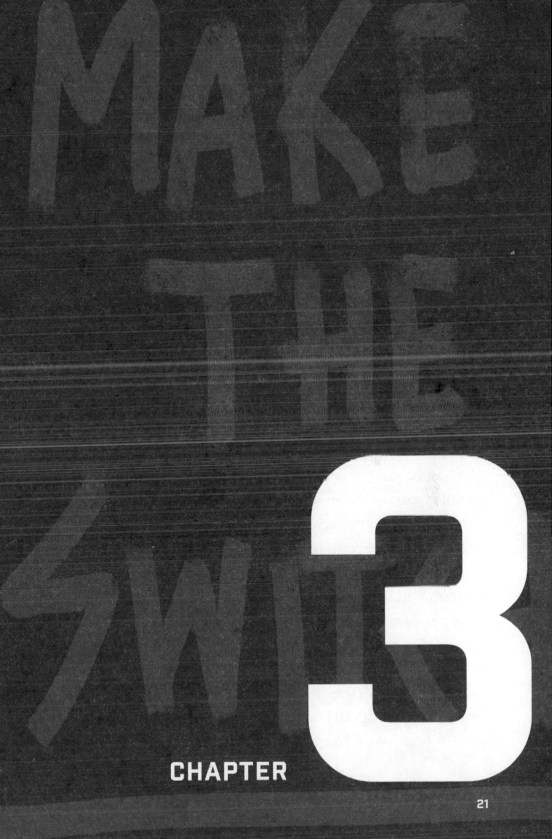

MAKE THE SWITCH

CHAPTER 3

If you've ever felt underqualified, you're in good company. The more I meet the heroes and generals of our time and the more I read God's Word, the more I find this is a common denominator in the lives of the called. Salvation came at an early age—to be honest, I don't have the date marked in my Bible like so many others I meet, but I did get saved. I kind of grew up under the pew. My mom and dad were on the worship team of our local church. I can remember them singing for hours and practicing old-time hymns. Every one of the songs seemed to have the same 2/4 beat on the drums. I grew up in a church that was filled with Holy Ghost encounters, a church that operated in the power of God. I was used to it; it was the norm. Throughout high school, I think I was trying to figure out if I really believed it for myself. I don't know if it was that I didn't believe it was real, I just didn't see past salvation. I had made Jesus my Savior, but I had no clue that I had to make Him Lord. But when I was 17, I said yes to Jesus and the plan He had for my life.

On a mission trip at 16 years of age to Mexico, the Lord wrecked me with a vision. As we sat around a campfire one night after the day's activities of loving on an orphanage, I had a vision, almost like an out-of-body experience. I was brought to a closed door, and on the front of the door it read "Destiny." Excited, I attempted to open the door. As I twisted the door-knob, the door was stuck, so I pulled harder, and finally the door opened. On the other side of the door was my girlfriend. She stood in such a way that I could not see around her. With a giant smile on her face, she stared at me. I must have had a fearful look on my face because she began asking me if everything was okay. When I woke from the vision, it was clear. To see all that

God had for me, I needed to remove this relationship. Without wasting any time, I called her cell phone and could not reach her. I then told some leaders in the group what had happened to me. I made one of those teenage vows with the Lord that when I got back home, I would do what I needed to do. But when I got home, sure enough, all the feelings came back, and I couldn't bear to break her heart. I wrote off the vision as a weird dream, and I convinced myself that it wasn't God.

Life went on, and when I was 17 years old, two of our classmates were killed in a head-on collision with a drunk driver. Their funeral was one of the most difficult days for the entire high school. I ended up close to the front row. Another student had told the mother of one of the young men who passed away that I was a Christian and that her son and I had a class together. So, right before the ceremony she asked me if I would pray peace over the crowd at the end. I got to the microphone, and it was a moment that every young Christian dreams of, their entire school at their attention, all their hearts wondering where they would spend eternity, wondering if they would ever see their friends again, mourning the loss of the ones that they had just seen the day before. As I grabbed the mic, I could have easily shared with the entire crowd about the Jesus I grew up with, the Jesus I had heard countless sermons about. I could have shared that He is a comforter when you're hurting. This moment could have been the moment that I had prayed about many times in my youth service when I'd pray, "God, send me. I'll go tell them about You." I wish I could say that I shared the Gospel with the crowd that day, but I didn't; fear overtook me. I heard its voice say, "You're not living it anyways." So instead I said a nice Christian prayer and took my seat.

Later that evening, a guy who grew up just down the block from my family's house went out to party to forget about his pain. He, his brother, and a few friends ended up at a local country spot where people go to get wasted. Supposedly, he was intoxicated and when he went to leave, he put his car in reverse instead of drive. The car rammed into a telephone pole. When he woke up from being knocked unconscious, he looked around in the car. Everyone had been knocked out, the windows were shattered, and blood was everywhere. In a drunken stupor, filled with pain, thinking he had killed everyone in the car, while still dealing with the pain from the day before, he made a split-second decision and wandered to the railroad tracks. It's all speculation and no one can prove what truly took place that night, but he died. Some say he took his life; others say he just got hit by the train. The train conductor said he blew his horn as many times as possible. Either he was in a daze, or he was bent on ending it all; no one can be sure.

I lost a great friend that night to a meaningless death. I remember every day of my senior year driving over those tracks, and every time I would weep. I felt like I could have done something, but I didn't. I felt like I was partly to blame. I had been too full of fear to step out and share hope with him, not even a day before. If I would have just rallied up 30 seconds of courage, what would have changed? What would have happened if I would have shared that Jesus didn't die to leave us in our fear and our pain and our shame, but that He became sin so that we would have freedom?

One day about a month after the incident, I was driving over those railroad tracks. I had driven over them every day after school; it seemed like hundreds of times. But this time was different. I heard a voice inviting me to come down the tracks. I pulled my car over and walked the tracks for what seemed like hours. Somehow I ended up at the place where he had died. I knew because his mom had set up a cross with rosary beads on it. I'll never forget falling at the cross, crying my eyes out, feeling so guilty and ashamed. I thought, *I could have given them hope, but because of fear I didn't. Now he is gone.* Then I heard the same voice that told me to walk down the train tracks say, "Jeremy, I'm the God of the second chance. That's what My cross represents, that every time death crosses you off at the path, I've come to give you life." I said, "If You're the God of the second chance, I want that second chance. If You give me a chance to tell people about You, I won't let You down again." That day I made the decision that from that point on, Jesus would not just be my Savior, He would be the Lord of my life. I didn't know what to do next, so I just did the first thing I knew God had asked of me. I drove straight to my girlfriend's house and did what I should have done two years earlier. I cried a lot of tears that day, but there is nothing like making Him Lord. I felt alive for the first time. The Bible began to speak to me. The pages were like food to my hungry soul. Obedience had its rewards, and the greatest of them was relationship with this God I heard about my whole life.

> I'M THE GOD OF THE SECOND CHANCE. THAT'S WHAT MY CROSS REPRESENTS, THAT EVERY TIME DEATH CROSSES YOU OFF AT THE PATH, I'VE COME TO GIVE YOU LIFE.

Soon after, they announced at church that we were starting an internship at my youth ministry, and I knew it was what I had to do. I canceled my plans to go to a four-year college. I had a dream of being an architect, but it was not God's dream. The old plans just seemed to not matter anymore. This new yes to Jesus transformed all my other responses to His voice. It was always "yes" from now on. This was no longer my life. When I was in charge of it, I kept messing it up. I was finally handing Him the pen back. He authored it, so now I was looking for Him to finish it. I joined the internship, and it was awesome and horrible all at the same time. I had to face the real me. I had never grown that much in my entire life. My youth pastor became not only my spiritual coach, but also my best friend. Years later, he would be the one to introduce me to my wife and help me plan our first date. I never knew that even though he and I had such a great beginning, our relationship would end in a horrible way. About three years into my internship, the senior pastor called me into his office. "Jeremy," he said with tears in his eyes, "your youth pastor resigned today. We found out recently that he was living in sin and had a moral failure. The woman who this took place with is no one you know, and we are working to restore him. Tonight, we have to tell the youth ministry. You're the only one I know who has access to the students' hearts. Jeremy, my own son and daughter attend that youth ministry. So, tonight, after we tell them, I want you to speak. Just bring a simple message of hope and help them make it through this."

I was in shock. First of all, I was dealing with the pain of just hearing about my pastor, my boss, my friend, and my hero. There's no way this man could have done this. It was so wrong. I was filled with anger, rage, hurt, and disappointment. Instantly, all the memories flooded my mind —everything he had asked me to do, every message, every encouraging word, yet this was who he was. This would teach me real forgiveness for the first time, the same forgiveness Jesus gave me at the cross I now had to extend to this man. I'll never forget sitting with his wife and seeing the forgiveness and love in her eyes. As a woman whose husband had just walked out on her, she said, "Jeremy, if I forgive him, you have to forgive him. Don't throw away the things he taught you because those words weren't from him but ultimately from the Lord. Run, but don't run away; run even harder after purity. The greatest thing that can happen to you is that you make it to the end of this and still love Jesus." That day, I forgave him for the hurt in my heart because of her encouragement. What a champion of a woman she was to walk in love like that.

I remember sitting at a Burger King later that afternoon thinking, *I have never preached a sermon.* In fact, I didn't think God would ever ask me to do this, at least not in this way, under this kind of circumstance. I ended up calling my wife Christy's dad, Pastor Glen Berteau. When he was a young youth pastor, his boss had done the same type of thing. I knew if anyone could help me, it would be him. As soon as I got a hold of him, he began to listen to my cries over the phone. I laid out all my hurts and fears. Then, with his words, he calmed me down and gave me a message to speak. I scribbled the message on a Burger King napkin, every point and every Scripture. Just when I started feeling better about what I would say that night, Pastor Glen asked me to rip up the napkin. I was so confused. He had just given me an entire message, and now he wanted me to rip it up. He said, "There's a better one inside of you. I just wanted you to know I could give you one, but God already put one inside you. You have been built for this moment. You just have to switch your fear." I said, "I don't understand." "Alright, close your eyes," he said. "You're on a street corner next to a main intersection in the middle of nowhere. In the blink of an eye, two cars both miss the stop signs and collide. It's a head-on collision, and immediately the cars erupt into flames. You start running away from the flames so you will not be engulfed in them. As you're running away, you're thinking that everyone in the car is dead and hoping that you make it through this moment. But then, you hear a sound coming from behind you in one of the cars; it's the cries of a baby. Both cars are on fire. What do you do?" I said, "I turn around and run back to the car." He stopped me. "Wait, why would you go back to the car?" "What do you mean, 'Why would I go back to the car?'" He said, "You don't know how to save a baby out of a burning car. You've never done it. You've never been trained. What if you finally get the baby out and it dies in your arms because you don't know what to do? Oh wait, unless the fear of running in is less than the fear of running away. Switch your fear."

THE FEAR OF THE RIGHT PERSON OR THE RIGHT THINGS IS YOUR GREATEST WEAPON AGAINST FEAR ITSELF.

The weight of that revelation hit me like a ton of bricks, and for the next 30 minutes, he explained to me that there had been a car wreck, spiritually. There were people that had casualties from something they couldn't control. They had been in the backseat of an absent-minded driver, and now they were crying for help, wondering if anybody would come to their rescue. Then he said, "Jeremy, tonight if you don't speak, people will become casualties of another man's misjudgment. This is what you were born for. Go rip them out of the car and give them life." Thus began something I will do for the rest of my life—preach the Gospel like a dying man preaches to other dying men. I must preach so that people would receive eternal life. I can't say the years of preaching have been easy, or that I haven't had to study. I'm not saying that every time there's already a sermon in me, or that I was never afraid again. What I can say is that Jesus does not leave you running into the burning car alone. If you want to be next to Jesus, you will be close to the hurting, rescuing the broken. This is what I live my life for, to say "yes" to Him one more day. It's time to switch your fear. Change your internal voice, and switch your fear. Fear always tries to focus us on the wrong fear. The fear of man, rather than the fear of the Lord. The fear of the right person, or the right things, is your greatest weapon against fear itself. Instead of, "What if I run in? What could happen?" I had to switch my fear to, "What if I ran away? What could happen?" I had to switch the narrative in my self-talk. I wasn't called to cower, but to be courageous. However, when you look at the options, I was scared of the lesser of the two fears. With this tactic against fear, I was quickly able to face the lesser of my fears. Regret comes when we look back over our lives and wish we would have chosen the opposite path than we chose. It won't always be the easier path, but when you switch the internal dialogue, you will quickly know the godly one. Which will usually be the one less traveled and narrow, but will always lead to life.

THE
CHOSEN

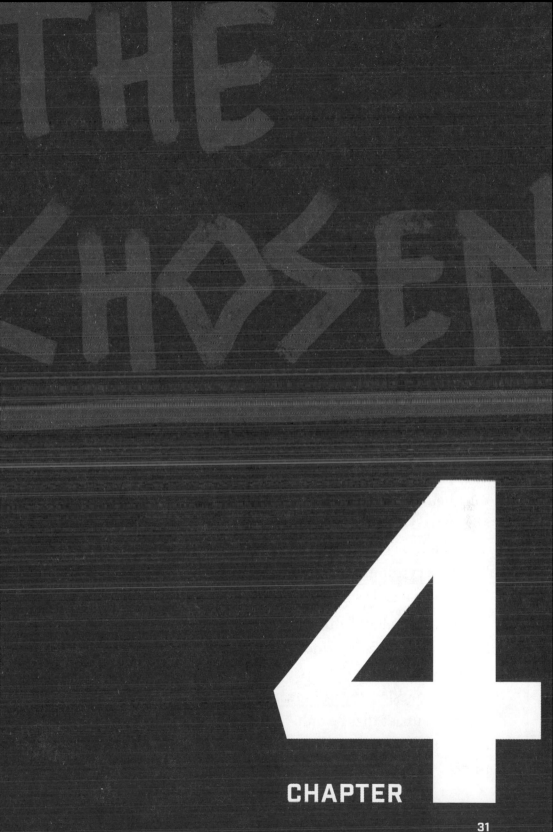

THE
KHOSEN

4

CHAPTER

The fear of being chosen often comes because of the price of standing alone or being the first. Although it's uncomfortable, this is by God's design. When I look at the disciples Jesus chose, they seem so random, so out of the box, like He wasn't even thinking. Was it random selection? Did it happen by chance? Were they just in the right place at the right time? Was it just a mass invite, and they were the only ones who said yes?

I think we get lost in the how, why and who; what He was trying to say to us is that every life has an assignment. As I looked into the lives of the disciples, I realized that Jesus did not pick them by accident. He did not randomly throw out "follow Me." The ones He said that to, were the ones who were called to respond to it. Not everybody He called embraced the call. Just because His invite is there does not mean we will answer. The Bible says that "many are called, but few are chosen" (Matt. 22:14 NKJV). I think few are chosen because few have chosen to say yes to Him. If we don't see the Scripture like this, we may believe that being chosen removes our choice from the equation. This was not the case for those who followed Christ. They had to choose to answer the call. They had to choose to leave everything. They had to choose, in times of popularity and times of isolation, to follow Jesus. We must do the same.

When you look at the Bible, you realize that not one of the heroes of faith was in competition with another; all of them were simply walking out their assignments. Did you know that Jeremiah prophesied during the same time as Ezekiel? We never see Jeremiah upset that he didn't get to prophesy about the Valley of the Dry Bones. No, he was too busy doing what he was called to do. We never see Moses and Aaron in an argument about who gets to hold the staff. When the Israelites were attacked by the Amalekites at Rephidim, Moses is given the instruction from God that he is to stand on the hill with the staff of God in his hand. Joshua is instructed by Moses to remain in the valley. We don't see Joshua wanting the hill and Moses wanting the valley. They knew they had a place, and they weren't worried about what place each other had. It was almost as if they were so consumed with their own assignments that they had no time to play the comparison game. Jesus chose the disciples in this exact way. He picked them based on assignment and call. They were destined to receive that call. There would've been nothing they could have done, or not done, to erase that call.

Some of the disciples' stories blow my mind. One of my favorites is when they were leaving the crowd in a boat and went across the sea. In the middle of the journey, while Jesus was fast asleep on the stern of the boat, a mighty squall broke out. The storm was literally ripping the boat to shreds. Jesus, the One who walked on water, multiplied fish, healed a blind man, and raised the dead, was on the boat. He was in the boat, yet they were freaked out and full of fear. They woke Jesus up, and I imagine Him wiping the sleep from His eyes, looking at the bow of the ship, and saying these three words: "Peace, be still" (Mark 4:39 NKJV). Instantly the storm died down. Then, He said this statement to them (almost as if He was irritated that they'd woken Him up from His sleep): "Why are you so fearful? How is it that you have no faith?" (v. 40 NKJV). In Matthew's account of the story, Jesus says, "You of little faith, why are you so afraid?" (Matt. 8:26). It's as if He was looking at them thinking, "Did you really think we were going to die in the storm?" He was saying, "My purpose is greater than the storm." Can you imagine the disciples as they sat back in the boat wondering what He would say next, alarmed and almost offended at His words, but mostly shocked at His power over the storm?

My favorite thought on this is that He was irritated that they woke Him up to handle this, almost as if when He said, "You of little faith," He was saying, "Why are you asking Me to do something you could have handled? You have power over this storm based on your proximity to Me, and the fact that you are walking in your call." This story could have been titled, "The Time the Disciples Calmed the Storm." Just like when Peter walked on water, when you don't realize who He is, you don't fully realize who you are and your place in the story.

When I was a kid, my favorite movie was *The NeverEnding Story*. The plotline of the movie is amazing. This misfit of a kid wanders into an old bookstore and sees an old stoic man reading a book. When he asks him about the book, the man pretty much says, "Oh, this book is too much for you to handle." When the man isn't looking, the main character grabs the book and runs out, goes to the creepy attic at school, and can't help but read the book. He finds out that the characters are real and can hear him. Sometimes, as he is reading, he shouts and his voice echoes in the story. I think this relates to us. Here we are reading the Bible, hanging over these moments, thinking this book is one-dimensional, but heaven is leaning over in this moment. Can you see the angels almost shouting out to the future heroes in their immature state, "Do you know who you are?" I feel like we forget that the pages of our lives are being written that same way. We are so fast to say, "Man, why did you guys wake up Jesus? Did you really think it was going to end like that?" Yet we sit in the midst of our storms shaking God with our prayers, wondering where He is in our daily storms. Heaven is shouting out to us, "Do you know who you are and the power you have been given? Speak to the storm!"

Jesus rebuked the disciples, rebuked the wind and the waves, and it was completely calm. I can imagine it was so calm that the boat creaked on the still waters, and on the faces of the disciples were horror, fear, and relief all at the same time as they realized once again who they were with. When they finally got to land, they arrived in the region of the Gerasenes, and a man from the tombs came running after them. Let's read it together:

> *They came to the other side of the sea, into the region of the Gerasenes. When He got out of the boat, immediately a man from the tombs with an unclean spirit met Him. He lived among the tombs; and no one was able to bind him anymore, not even with a chain, because he had often been bound with shackles and chains, and the chains had been torn apart by him and the shackles broken in pieces; and no one was strong enough to subdue him. Constantly, night and day, he was screaming among the tombs and in the mountains, and cutting himself with stones. Seeing Jesus from a distance, he ran up and bowed down before Him; and shouting with a loud voice, he said, "What business do You have with me, Jesus, Son of the Most High God? I implore You by God, do not torment me!" For He had already been saying to him, "Come out of the man, you unclean spirit!" And He was asking him, 'What is your name?" And he said to Him, "My name is Legion, for we are many." And he begged*

Him earnestly not to send them out of the region (Mark
5:1–10 NASB).

This man could not be contained. The town had tried to
chain him, but he had broken the chains. I imagine the chains
clinking as he ran. He was dirty, grungy, and might have had
multiple personalities using different voices. As he ran toward
the disciples, he yelled to Jesus far enough off, "What business
do You have with me, Jesus, Son of the Most High God?" It is
interesting that even the enemy knows who Jesus is. It's crazy
that the disciples were just in the storm a few minutes earlier,
and they had forgotten who He was, yet the enemy had not
forgotten. Although we may forget how powerful God is while
we are in the storm, the enemy knows that at the name of
Jesus, things shift. The evil spirit in the man shouted at Jesus,
"I implore You by God, do not torment me!" Then, "he begged
Him earnestly not to send them out of the region."

The word *region* sticks out to me there. The demons didn't
want to leave the region. My number-one question is, why
were they so specific with their request to stay in the region?
Secondly, why did they feel like they had bargaining power
with God? Even later, after the people saw that Jesus had
delivered the man, they begged Jesus to leave the region.
However, what they didn't realize was that now Jesus had
a disciple in the region who would spread the testimony of
what He had done.

*And they began to beg Him to leave their region. And
as He was getting into the boat, the man who had been
demon-possessed was begging Him that he might
accompany Him. And He did not let him, but He said to*

him, "Go home to your people and report to them what
great things the Lord has done for you, and how He had
mercy on you." And he went away and began to proclaim
in Decapolis what great things Jesus had done for him;
and everyone was amazed (Mark 5:17–20 NASB).

As you can see in the Scripture, this new disciple, formerly
known as Legion, tried to leave with Jesus, but Jesus tells him
instead to go home and share his testimony. Oftentimes, when
Jesus healed someone, He would tell them to do the same (i.e.
the man with leprosy, the man lowered through the roof). Jesus's
famous last words to someone after they were healed were "Go
home." In other words, "Go back to the place where you left
broken or that broke you, and I will use you to bring wholeness
to others through the wholeness I've brought to your life."

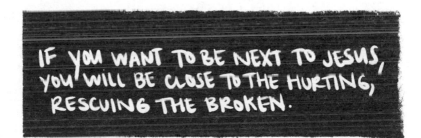

IF YOU WANT TO BE NEXT TO JESUS,
YOU WILL BE CLOSE TO THE HURTING,
RESCUING THE BROKEN.

Jesus now had a disciple who would reach the whole region.
Connecting to what I previously said, all of the disciples were
chosen and given an assignment to take over their regions.
This is exactly what Jesus did with the disciples. Andrew, Peter,
James, and John were fishermen. Matthew was a tax collector
for the Roman government. Simon was a zealot, which was a
political anarchist. We don't know the professions of Philip, Bar-
tholomew, Thomas, Thaddeus, or James, but we do know that

Paul, who later became an apostle, was a Pharisee and worked in politics. The disciples were from varying backgrounds, and their personalities were extremely different. God had chosen them to be the first of many to accept Christ, and to use them to redeem regions. Maybe you were the first in your family to accept Christ. Sometimes being the first, you feel alone, misunderstood, and isolated. You may wonder, *When is everyone else going to receive what I have?* But you must remember that since you're the first, God is going to use you to reach the most. Just as Jesus wasn't worried about leaving the region because He had left the man who was formerly named Legion there, He had left the disciples to spread the name of Jesus wherever they went. God is not nervous about your family, your school, or your workplace, because He left you there. You were chosen to be fearless there. Don't let the fear of being first, or alone, drive you away. If you're the only one, your value doesn't go down—your value goes up. You have been hand-chosen by God to be the first of the whole region. Small doesn't intimidate God. God can do amazing things with just one. One man, named Moses, set millions free from slavery. One man, named David, declared war on the giants. One woman, named Esther, decided the fate of a nation. One small boy's lunch fed fifteen thousand on a hillside, and one cross changed my eternity. What could God do with one? Better yet, what could God do if you're the first? First in your family to get saved. First in your field to walk in righteousness. God loves the one and He loves the first. If you have been saying, "I'm the only one," you may need to rethink that and turn your complaint into praise. God chose you for the entire region. Don't take it flippantly that God has eyes for you and put you first. Don't let fear tell you you're alone because it won't be long until God turns a spark into a forest fire through your life.

PURSUE
EXCELLENCE

5

CHAPTER

Say yes with what you have; don't wait for what you don't have. Fear will tell you to wait because you can't compete at the level yet, but faith calls you forward. We must know that God knows what you have and what you don't. I have found, God is more concerned with availability than ability. Our willingness to trust Him is how we move forward without all the skills or the answers. God called Gideon to go in the strength he had. Don't wait for one day; begin today with the strength you do have. That doesn't mean you can't be excellent in what God is calling you to do. Being excellent is simply doing the best with what you have. Fear will keep you waiting to make sure you're ready to keep up, trying to be as good as…

Now, with social media, every idea, every creative concept, and every filtered moment is on display. We scroll daily through the highlight reels while living our unedited reality. No matter what you're pursuing, you can find someone doing it better, faster, or bigger than you. Fear puts us in a rat race trying to keep up, making sure we're not behind, making sure our message is expressed in a way that is current with what's happening. Fear tells us our life is about competition. The problem with competition is that, in actuality, we are in a solo race. Throughout my life, I've added imaginary runners to the race with me—my peers, my heroes, my family—all of them become my competitors. It's almost as if, as long as I was ahead of them, I felt better about myself. It was almost like others were my gauge to measure if I was succeeding or failing. The problem with competition is that even when you're ahead, it's stressful. You're constantly looking in your rearview mirror, making sure no one is catching up, because the only way to feel good about yourself is to be a few steps ahead. If we are trying to be relevant with the people around us and the world, we will always be striving for something and never resting in where God has us. We will miss what's right in front of us because we are chasing something that was never ours to hold. How do we keep up with the Joneses, or that super mom, photoshopped abs, soaring career, fastest-growing church, the marriage that never has problems? We can't keep up, so one more year we fail, feeling worse about ourselves than we did before.

Here's the thing: I don't believe God ever called us to be as good as... to reach our world. Throughout the Bible I see that God tells us to be excellent. To be excellent is different from being as good as. To be as good as, you're always missing some ingredient you need to move forward, and if you just have that one thing, you could succeed. Excellence is different. Being excellent is looking inside your arsenal at the things you have been given. Being excellent is asking the tough questions, such as, "Have I been faithful with what I've been given?" Moses was given a shepherd's staff yet called to be a deliverer. The picture of a deliverer in most people's minds would be someone wearing a crown, holding a sword, and having an army at their back. Moses didn't have those things, all he had was a word from God, his brother, and a shepherd's rod. It's amazing what God can do with a shepherd's rod. When he began to work with what he already had, God brought about excellence in his life. Excellence is about using what you have to its utmost potential. David did this with stones, Moses did this with the staff, and Mary did this with her womb. God is looking for those who will dig deep into what He's given them and be faithful, even if what they have feels small. When you walk in excellence, you stop thinking about what you don't have. Instead, you act from a place of knowing you have been given all you need. Being excellent takes creativity, it takes courage. It takes looking inside yourself to find the solution you already possess.

> GOD IS LOOKING FOR THOSE WHO WILL DIG DEEP INTO WHAT HE'S GIVEN THEM AND BE FAITHFUL EVEN IF WHAT THEY HAVE FEELS SMALL.

When we first started Fearless Church, we met on the beach with about seven people. We made a commitment that we would be excellent. We put a team over who would gather the wood, who would keep the fire going, and who would bring out the doughnuts (that was the most important job, really). Our associate pastor jokes that his first job at Fearless was "wind blocker." I know this doesn't exist in most churches, but most churches don't meet on the beach! It can get really windy in Southern California, so he went to Home Depot with a $30 gift card someone had given in the offering to gather all the supplies needed to block the wind. You should have seen the creativity that went into designing the first ever Fearless wind blocker. That's just it, right? All that God requires of us is that we use what we are given to the best of our ability.

Once we had outgrown the beach, we started renting various venues around town, mostly LA's top nightclubs. Even though our environment was more relevant with the latest gear, 30-foot LED wall, best sound system, plush seating, even good air conditioning, our days on the beach were actually more "excellent" than our first days in the nightclubs. More is always more. We had the beach down; we had figured out what we needed to do. But the new nightclub location was more than any of us understood. It took us years to get to the same level of excellence as our later days on the beach. But we still pursued excellence with what we had and what we knew. God helped us grow from there.

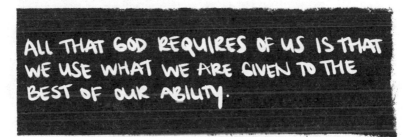

ALL THAT GOD REQUIRES OF US IS THAT WE USE WHAT WE ARE GIVEN TO THE BEST OF OUR ABILITY.

Are you working from a place of relevance or a place of excellence? I believe God honors excellence. As soon as you're excellent on one level, you graduate to the next. Many of us want to get to the next level. We think we're going to do it by keeping up with those next to us, then we wonder why we're in a holding pattern for the rest of our lives. At the end of our lives, when we meet the Lord, He will ask, "What did you do with what I gave you?" What will you say? "Lord I would have done...but I didn't have..."?

Never let fear of what you don't have keep you from moving forward. The fearless life is all about giving God room to work. If you can do it all, why would you need God. God will give you a call based on Him as the major factor in the equation. God will always make room for Himself.

You can embrace your call today; tell fear its idea of tomorrow is too late. Fear loves tomorrow; it wins a battle it has already lost with one word: tomorrow. Choose to stop letting it win today. God loves now, because it's the now that leads to tomorrow. The now call is where God gets the glory in your life. It's where you thank Him for what He has given you and trust Him in what He hasn't. Never again will we let fear decide our future by holding hostage our present. God is proud of who He made you to be; who you are is enough. He doesn't want a plastic you, what you believe is the perfect cleaned-up you. He wants you in all your process and all your problems, that is what gets Him the most glory. God made us unique; it's our uniqueness that brings the real joy to the family and call of God.

> *But thanks be to God, who always leads us as captives in Christ's triumphal procession and uses us to spread the aroma of the knowledge of him. For we are to God the pleasing aroma of Christ among those who are being saved and those who are perishing. To the one we are an aroma that brings death; to the other, an aroma that brings life. And who is equal to such a task? Unlike so many, we do not peddle the word of God for profit. On the contrary, in Christ we speak before God with sincerity, as those sent from God* (2 Corinthians 2:14–17).

We are not victorious because we won, we are victors because He has already won the victory. For many years, I found myself warring in a battle that was already won. You have already won the battle with fear through Christ Jesus.

This is good news, we've already won! We no longer have to fight to win, we just have to remember that He has already won. We have to look beyond the facts, and let the truth of His triumph speak. "And having disarmed the powers and authorities, he made a public spectacle of them, triumphing over them by the cross" (Col. 2:15). His triumph has caused us to triumph. "Now thanks be unto God, which always causeth us to triumph in Christ, and maketh manifest the savour of his knowledge by us in every place" (2 Cor. 2:14 KJV).

The Bible calls us to triumph. The Bible calls us not to win the victory, but to celebrate the victory we have already won. Killing Jesus on the cross was the worst decision the devil ever made, because when Jesus gave up His life, He gave us a second chance. When He rose from the grave, He publicly displayed His greatness over death. King Jesus defeated the devil, and we continue to defeat him. If we are going to live in triumph, we have to stop giving the devil so much credit.

Years ago, triumph is what happened after a battle. The victorious king would humiliate his defeated foe by stripping him naked and tying him and his officials to the back of his chariot. In the triumphal procession, the king and his family would ride through the streets proclaiming victory as the enemy was dragged behind the chariot. The crowds filled the streets, praising the king for his great power. Jesus is that King. He has picked us up out of the muck and mire and has given us a seat next to Him in the chariot. He wants us to remember and to celebrate His victory over the enemy. It's our job to remember, but for far too long we've given the enemy too much power. We've allowed ourselves to be influenced by the voices we hear behind the chariot. The enemy whispers lies in our ears in efforts to remove us from our victorious position. When we allow him to feed us those lies, we begin to drag along with him, fighting for the seat we already have. What was once a powerful relationship becomes the drag of religion.

Only family rides in the chariot. As family, God is not only King and Lord, but Dad. The Bible tells us that He isn't just any dad but a good father. This Father is in love with His children. That includes you. God's love for you isn't based on performance but sonship. Since you can't overperform or underperform, His love remains the same at all times. In short, He doesn't love you at a level one or two when you have been bad and a nine or ten when you've been perfect. You are loved at level ten at all times, not because you are good, but because He's good and you are His. Let me say it louder for those in the back row of religion today. HE DOESN'T ENDURE US; HE ENJOYS US! To understand this, God's love has to continue to wash over us like giant waves until we realize His love is more powerful than our greatest defeat or greatest strength.

"THIS BATTLE IS NOT FOR YOU TO FIGHT; TAKE YOUR POSITION, STAND STILL, AND SEE THE VICTORY OF THE LORD ON YOUR BEHALF, O JUDAH AND JERUSALEM." DO NOT FEAR OR BE DISMAYED; TOMORROW GO OUT AGAINST THEM, AND THE LORD WILL BE WITH YOU.

2 CHRONICLES 20:17

GOD SEES
THE ONE

CHAPTER **6**

One of my favorite stories is the time a stormtrooper got saved at Fearless. He may have dressed as a stormtrooper, but his name is Gabe. You never know what you're going to get when you have church in a nightclub in downtown Los Angeles. When we first met Gabe, we had no clue just how awesome he was. He was amazing as a person, but we had no clue that he was a real stormtrooper. To become a real stormtrooper, you have to be approved by the Official Star Wars Fan Club. Gabe had an official number and everything. We met him on the streets of downtown LA while hosting our first ever block party. We gathered all the downtown residents—the homeless, the hipsters, the businessmen. What a crowd it was! We blocked off a parking lot, put up a bounce house and a mechanical bull, and gave out free food. Pretty irresistible, if you ask me!

We gathered quite the crowd simply by sending a smoke-flavored chicken aroma through the atmosphere of downtown. We were having a blast just loving on our community. During the outreach, I got up on a small platform and shared why we were doing this. I told the crowd how God brought us there to love more and fear less, and that our church was named Fearless. The God of love told us to love people until they asked why. When I got off the stage, I knew I would get a lot of whys. One in particular came through our good friend Gabe. Gabe was a hardcore punk rocker. He had a punk rock jacket, a nose ring, and a bright pink mohawk that stood about 2 feet tall above his head. When Gabe approached me, I was able to share with him the why behind our love for the community. I explained that Jesus first loved us, and that this love wasn't from us but was the love of Jesus displayed through us. That day in the middle of downtown, Gabe surrendered and turned his life over to the perfect love of Jesus. I invited him to the church service we were having the next morning. I didn't know if he would come, or if he was just being cordial, but it seemed like what happened in him that day was real.

The next morning, I looked for Gabe, searching for the pink mohawk as I opened the service. No pink mohawk. But halfway through the service I noticed that Gabe was there. He had been in the back row the whole time. The reason I couldn't see his pink mohawk was because he had a hood on. I ran up to him, and when I saw his eyes, I could tell something was wrong. "Gabe, what's wrong man? Why are you so down? I'm so pumped you're here." He said, "Yesterday after we met, I failed God. I went and got high again on the things He just forgave me of. How could I be so rude to Him? As soon as He gives me life, I go back to death." As the worship team played, I began to explain to Gabe that the journey with Jesus is just that, a journey, and that God wasn't mad at him; He was madly in love with him. I encouraged Gabe and told him that I was proud of him for even coming to church. I said, "Gabe, how can I make you more comfortable?" Gabe reluctantly responded, "The only way I know I feel comfortable is in my suit." I figured he was talking about a three-piece suit. Boy, was I wrong. I said, "Gabe, anytime you want to wear your suit, you rock that suit."

The service went on. I preached my sermon and gave an altar call, inviting people to receive Jesus. A few raised their hands, we cheered, and we prayed together. At the end there was a moment when I felt from the Holy Spirit that there was one more person who needed to respond. I extended my altar call again, and out of nowhere a stormtrooper came hopping down to the front from the back of the nightclub. This shy voice coming out of the mask responded to the call saying, "It's me, it's me, it's me." I was halfway in shock and a little confused, and so was the audience. People immediately began to pull out their phones to capture this unusual moment. I thought to myself, "Only in LA would we have this final person be a real-life storm-trooper." I could see security wondering what they should do. "Was this person harmless, or did he have plans to do something violent? Was he plotting something with his fake gun?" Once he got closer, he began to remove his white helmet, and to my surprise, it was Gabe! Instantly it hit me, "Oh, that's your suit." He had gone home for the rest of the message and arrived right on time to hear my second call. I said, "Well, I guess God is turning even the dark side to the light today. Next will be a Sith Lord or Darth Vader." Only in LA, only my Jesus.

What an amazing journey it is to allow the love of God to love on people through you. God isn't mad at us, He loves us with extreme love. He loves us just how we are, and it's that love that beckons us to continue to be more like Him. You need to hear this today: You bring joy to God's heart. He will never reject you. His call is irrevocable. There is nothing you can do to remove it.

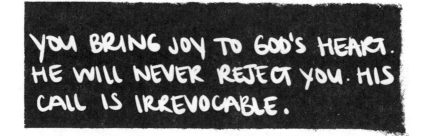

A Big Mac, Fries, and a Coke

Gabe's salvation was not the first time I've seen Him meet a son in power. His eyes are not on crowds; they're on the hurting, broken sons and daughters hidden in every crowd. Ministers get it mixed up when we like crowds and Jesus loves His kids in the crowd. The lengths He goes to rescue just one often blows my mind.

One of my favorite examples of this was revealed to me through a guy named Cardboard.

Rewind to my early days of ministry way before Fearless Church. After a few years of youth ministry, I went away to complete college. Because I had been in full-time ministry, I couldn't help but see the hurt and pain on my own college campus. Those who had shown up with dreams of changing the world grew apathetic while consuming a steady diet of homework, theological debates, video games, and discovering new music on their illegally downloaded programs. In many ways, our Christian Bible college looked no different than a secular campus. These people were just better at hiding what was really going on in their lives. It broke my heart to see that those studying the Word so diligently didn't know the love on its pages. One day it hit me, I wasn't there to just get a degree. Ultimately, I was there to show the people around me who they were again. I knew that having a job in the Kingdom would give them purpose again. I had seen this work with teenagers, so I figured it must also work with college students. Then, that purpose drove discipleship. So, as I would travel and speak in the area to different youth ministries, I would invite along whomever from school wanted to go. The first time a crew went with me, God touched them as they prayed for students and watched their lives change through the Gospel. It was as if they remembered the reason they were born—to go into all the earth and make disciples. They saw themselves in those teenagers' eyes. Later that year, we began going out so much that Intense Ministries was formed. I wrote a drama to give the students jobs. Playing a role was a way for them to find some belonging. One of the guys in the drama team was a dancer, so he asked to start writing some dances. This pulled in a whole new crew of people. My roommate loved filming videos, so we started making videos that went along with the dances and dramas. Before we knew it, we were meeting every Tuesday night to rehearse the major production we had written purely out of the thought that "these people need something to do." The funny thing is, we had nowhere to bring it. After it was done, I began to ask God what He wanted to do with it.

There are so many stories I could tell you about my time with Intense Ministries. When 9/11 happened, the dad of one of the girls in our ministry paid for all of us to fly to New York to minister on the streets. One time, the motor home we were given to travel in caught on fire in front of a gas station. In the aftermath of fixing that motorhome, an angel (I totally think it could have been!) pulled over on the side of the road and used gum to fix a pipe that was leaking. I remember the time we laid hands on the broken engine of our truck, and even though mechanics told us it would never run again, it started. My favorite story has to be Cardboard's, though.

This time we joined with another ministry on the streets of Hollywood. They did an outreach there every year, and they blocked off the streets and gave out something for free, which of course would gather a crowd. This year, the free items were hot dogs and Sunny Select sodas. It worked; over 5,000 people had gathered by noon! The street was packed. Our drama team and dance team performed, and then it was my time to speak. I also can't forget to mention that I had a fresh set of dreads. At the last minute, the guy who played Jesus in all of our plays canceled, so I volunteered to get dreads so I could play Jesus. After playing Jesus in the drama, I walked to the front of the stage. It hit me as I walked up there, how exciting this was. There were 5,000 people, most of them unbelievers, in Hollywood. It reminded me of the Book of Acts—the church shows up with God's power and people gather, and are changed for all of eternity.

I couldn't wait to tell them about the love of Jesus. I got about three words into my testimony when something strange happened. My microphone began to cut out. Pretty soon it was going in and out to the point that people began laughing as I was speaking. I looked up at the sound guy. He looked just as frazzled as me, with sweat pouring down his head and his fingers frantically pressing every button. I looked at my teammates, who were praying. One elderly lady from the event even jumped on the stage and started putting anointing oil on the speakers and cables. I'm not sure that was the best idea, but hey, we were desperate. Over 5,000 people were waiting to hear the Gospel. We had planned this entire event for this moment. Surely God was going to show up and fix it. In that moment, every second felt like eternity. Two minutes went by, and then five, and then 10, 20, and by the time we hit 60 minutes, our faith had dwindled, and our hopes were crushed. People started leaving in droves, hundreds exiting the little space where we had gathered. As soon as they finished their hot dogs, they figured we weren't getting the sound system back on. I don't blame them.

I still remember the feeling as I sat on the edge of the stage. I was royally disappointed that God didn't show up. It was such a letdown to our team and all the volunteers who had worked so hard to see this event come to pass. I had seen God show up so many times before. I had seen Him restore vision, heal backs, and destroy cancer. He even supernaturally fixed our motor home. I knew He could do it, so why didn't He? I was so mad at God. I couldn't figure out why He would bring us all the way there for it to result in nothing, no advance of the Kingdom. *What a waste,* I thought. I got to such a low place while I sat on that stage that I said the stupidest thing I've probably ever said: "Fine, God. If You don't want them saved, then neither do I. You know what, God? I don't want a hot dog or Sunny Select soda. I want a Big Mac, a large fry, and a large Coke." I had been eyeing McDonald's the whole day. So, I began my journey across the street to buy my dinner and sulk. As I wandered over there, I tripped on something right in front of the door; this "something" was a person. An old, weathered man popped up and introduced himself. "The name's Cardboard," he shouted in an angry, don't-mess-with-me kind of way. I moved on and tried to ignore him, pretending like I didn't just trip over him. Growing up in a small town, we'd always been told there were some crazy people in LA, and this was my first encounter with one of them.

Seconds later, I opened the door at McDonald's, and the smell of the fries made me forget all about Cardboard. As I was ordering, I got a call from one of our team members saying we needed to clean up, so after my order was ready, I headed out the door. This time, I walked around Cardboard, who was back asleep, thank God. When I was about 10 feet from Cardboard, I heard the overwhelming voice of God for the first time. "Jeremy, go give your Big Mac, large fry, and Coke to Cardboard. You got that for him, not for you." So I did what any believer would have done in my shoes. I said, "Get behind me, satan, in the name of Jesus! You foul spirit, go back to where you belong." The voice just got louder and louder, and louder, though. I felt like if I were to eat one of the fries, a bolt of lightning might come from heaven and strike me down. Really though, it was intense. So, finally I went back to Cardboard. I was scared to wake him up, but God was not letting up on it. When he woke up and wiped the sleep from his eyes, he had no clue I was the guy he had yelled at earlier. He sat up, and the smell of urine and alcohol flooded my nostrils as he moved to hear what I was going to say. "Hello, Cardboard. My name is Jeremy. This may be strange, but I got you something—a Big Mac, a large fry, and a large Coke." I handed Cardboard the three items and began to walk away.

As I walked away, I thought nothing of what had just happened, except that God also took away my Big Mac, my large fry, and my Coke and gave it to Cardboard. My mind began to think like an orphan: "This must be punishment for my attitude earlier." As I was in my own victim mentality, I heard Cardboard yell to me from behind, "Who told you to give me this?" I wasn't sure why, but he was very disturbed about what just happened. In order to calm him down, I walked back toward him. "Is everything okay?" I asked. Looking me in the eyes, he asked again: "Who told you to give me this?" "Cardboard, you're never going to believe this, but here it goes. God told me to give it to you." When I said those words, Cardboard looked at me as if he had seen a ghost. He said, "It's you." "It's me," I responded. "It's you; you're the guy who was on stage." Then he asked me,

"How did you know?" "Know what?" I asked. He just looked up and then crumbled to the ground weeping and muttering under his breath, "There's no way, there's no way, there's no way." I finally calmed him down, and he began to explain to me what had happened.

"Let me reintroduce myself. My name is Samuel. I used to attend the church that put the outreach on that you are part of today. Four years ago, I lost my job, my wife lost her job, and we have two kids. After not being able to pay our rent for months, they finally evicted us. I wound up out here with my family on the street. I didn't know what to do, so I just started begging, and we popped in and out of shelters before ending up here. I built a shelter out of cardboard for my wife and kids, so the locals gave me a new name: Cardboard. After a few months out here, my wife and kids left me. Every year the church that I loved would come out to the streets and tell us how much they loved us, and would give us a meal. Then the next day, I would be out here alone again.

"Jeremy, I have to be honest; I've grown bitter, to the point that I didn't believe there was a God anymore. In fact, today as they began to set up their annual outreach, I heard a voice inside my head that said, 'God isn't real.' I couldn't get it to go away, so I just drank myself to sleep. When I woke up, it was still there. That's when the drama team was performing on stage. I just kept hearing the voice say, 'God's not real.' Then the voice told me to climb to the top of the building."

Cardboard pointed to a seven-story building next to where we were doing the outreach. The building had businesses on the first and second floors, but the rest of the floors looked like they had been boarded up and abandoned. He continued, "I climbed up to the top of the fifth floor. I went out to the window ledge where the fire escape was. I sat there, and then I heard the voice say, 'Jump. Life isn't worth living.' As I saw you coming to the front, I climbed to the end of the ledge, and right before I was about to leap, I heard another voice say, 'Samuel, ask Me for anything.' I remember getting angry. 'Not now, God; You can't be real. Okay, You have one shot. I don't want a hot dog or a Sunny Select soda. I'm going to go lay under my blanket, and I want that guy, the guy with the dreads, to bring me a Big Mac, a large fry, and a large Coke. I'll be waiting under my blanket.'" Then, his eyes began to tear up. "And here you are with a Big Mac, a large fry, and a large Coke."

That day, I didn't lead thousands in a sinner's prayer, but I did lead one; his name was Samuel, but the world called him Cardboard. I don't know what happened to Cardboard after that moment, but I do believe that he encountered God—not church, not religion, but the power of the living God that breaks all the rules to rescue His lost sheep. Then it hit me; God had planned this whole thing. The sound issue was not an accident or a malfunction. God took over the sound system. He shut it down, and there was nothing we could have done to get it back on. That day, I learned that God never makes a mistake. As I walked back to the event area, I saw things with new eyes. I saw the 300 volunteers cleaning up the mess that 5,000 people had left. It took hours just to get the streets back to the way they were. Wow! 300 people getting off work, arranging for babysitters, and driving through LA traffic. I mean, the permits it would've taken to block off the city streets in Hollywood, the weeks waiting for approval, the hundreds of emails back and forth. All the food that was donated, and what it took to get those donations. The 14 cooks that spent hours grilling hot dogs. However, the person we came for would not watch the drama or eat the hot dog or even stand in the blocked-off zone we had created. God did all of this through us not for 5,000, but for one. This one didn't even have a name anymore. He wasn't the mayor, he wasn't a celebrity, he wasn't a well-to-do family man. In fact, he had lost his family and was just trying to survive. I am overwhelmed by this reckless love of God. God doesn't see crowds; He sees the one. In fact, He's always seen the one. Maybe today you feel embarrassed like Gabe the storm-trooper or abandoned and forgotten like Cardboard. God both sees and loves you at your worst as if you were the only one. The Bible says, "But God demonstrates his own love for us in this: While we were still sinners, Christ died for us" (Rom. 5:8 NIV). He is not embarrassed of you or ghosting you. He gave His very life to redeem you at your worst. Let God break sin and shame today with His perfect love. God loves everyone from the drug addict stormtrooper to the lost homeless man named Cardboard. God has not forgotten you, because you are His kid. Let that destroy your fear today—God's eyes are on you today. He not only sees you, He adores you. He is not mad at you but madly in love with you. Not because you're perfect, but because you're His. Let that drive you to Him, not from Him.

GET A
STRONGER
SOURCE

CHAPTER **7**

God sees us, but we need to remember that man usually doesn't. We must always remember in this journey you can be chosen by God and be rejected by man. Rejection from man does not mean rejection from God, just as being chosen by man does not mean you have been chosen by God. In fact, we see that many times, the two are opposing. From the stories of Moses to David to Jesus, we can see that many times, being in heaven's hall of fame means being in Earth's hall of shame. As humans, we tend to choose people based on outward things, their popularity, for example, but God looks past this and chooses man based on the heart. Be cautious to not only choose who follows you based on the heart, but also who you follow.

Being a pastor has been one of the most challenging things I have walked through so far in the area of acceptance and rejection. Many times, when we think of walking with God, we think rejection is part of the job. At first thought, we think it means rejection from the world. Yes, this is a given. To the person in the world, what we are doing is some fairy tale. They imagine that we are chasing an invisible God who has us on a delusional roller coaster of religion. It makes sense that we would be rejected by the world.

As a young believer, signing up to be hated by the world was a given, and it was my first step to becoming more like Jesus. We don't have to work at being rejected. Being hated comes with the territory of walking with God. Strangely, it seems like some people work overtime trying to find more reasons to be persecuted. I have found that even when you love people from the heart, persecution will still come, and you don't have to search for it. However, in my opinion, that isn't the painful part. The difficulty comes when the rejection sources from those inside the house of God. It's easy when the attack comes from those who are in the world, as those moments usually push you closer to Jesus. The most heart-wrenching rejection I've experienced is the kind that comes from those who are in the faith.

On my journey to plant this church, I received several words from men and women about things God wanted to encourage me with. The one that stands out to me the most is when I was told that the first part of my ministry would be marked by creativity, and the second half would be marked by courage. I would need courage to face the hallways of Hollywood and the secularism of Los Angeles, but I would also need it for the corridors of the church. In the next season, I would be attacked from both ends, and I would need courage to move forward. I had no clue the number of times I would return to that word throughout my journey. Rejection from inside the walls of a family, or a church, will always be the most painful a man or woman could experience. However, even Jesus Himself faced this in extreme measures. Look at what Isaiah prophesied about Him:

> *He grew up before him like a tender shoot, and like a root out of dry ground. He had no beauty or majesty to attract us to him, nothing in his appearance that we should desire him. He was despised and rejected by mankind* (Isaiah 53:2–3a).

He was despised and rejected by men. The primitive root of the word despised is *bāzâ*, which means "to disesteem," which is by definition, "disdain." Look at the definition of *disdain*:

> The feeling that someone or something is unworthy of one's consideration or respect; contempt.

Jesus was rejected because He was considered unworthy of consideration or respect. I feel like I experience that on a daily basis. At times it's the truth of a fallen world; at other times it's my mind perceiving new relationships through past wounds, causing me to be skeptical of allowing anyone in. It is going to take courage for me to be rejected to this level.

Recently, I asked God why He allowed His Son to go through what He experienced, and then it became clear to me. He had to experience rejection and pain so that I would feel like He knew and understood me, and because I feel known, I allow Him greater access to my heart. Then God told me, "That's it! Now, why do you think I allow you to experience the same thing?" It was even clearer. I must be rejected so that the rejected will let me in. This isn't easy, especially when the rejection comes from the family of God. There are so many hurting and offended people in the house of God. I have found out that offended people love to cheer on each other's offenses. It's as if when there is someone new added to the ranks of offense, they all of a sudden become best friends. Is it real? Or, is it just that when others are offended, they feel right about their own bitterness? Righteousness, on the other hand, can stand alone; it needs no validation from others. Self-righteousness cannot. Look at your crowd. Who is surrounding you? Who is closest to you? They will affect your character, commitment, comments, and your call. Make sure they are cheering you on for the reason of getting closer to Jesus, not closer to proving them right. Offended people spend their lives proving that they're justified in being angry about being wronged. The single best weapon the enemy has built against us is to get us to pick up the rights we laid down when we gave our lives to the Lord. Offense spreads to those in close proximity. How much offense you tolerate in others around you will be a direct correlation to the offense inside you.

Isaiah goes on to say that Jesus was a man of sorrows, familiar with suffering, like one from whom people hide their faces (v. 3). Have you ever felt like people are hiding their true feelings about you? They don't have the decency to come and talk to you about what is really going on. Many offended people I come across tell the whole world about how they were wronged, but they never sit down with the person they felt wronged them with a genuine heart to mend it. If an offended person lets go of their offense, what else will justify them in their running? They will have to press deeper into the relationship. Their hurt has become their comfort zone and identity, so subconsciously they continue to look for more things that will hurt them. Life becomes about hurt instead of healing, fear instead of faith. The truth is, you will find whatever you're looking for. If you look through the lens of the victim, you will always be the victim. If you look through the lens of a victor, you will always be a victor. God is looking for some leaders to help remove people's lens of victimhood and release victory over their lives. You can listen and be sensitive to a victim as long as you listen and are sensitive to the Holy Spirit about their healing at the same time. This healing might come through confrontation, or a challenge, as well as soft words and listening.

The painful part of being a leader is that people will just cut you out of their lives without giving you a chance to hear about what hurt them until it's too late. This sometimes is after they have shared their hurt with many others, which makes it worse.

In any relationship, we must know that there will be moments of hurt, pain, and conflict, but we have to include grace in every relationship, even when it involves someone we greatly respect. In fact, just because we respect them doesn't mean they are not humans with flaws. Sometime,s we idolize people who we are only meant to honor. We have expected them to be as perfect as Jesus, and we have idolized them as if they were God. We've removed their humanity from the equation of the relationship, setting ourselves up for great disappointment. If you're alive and breathing, other humans will hurt you, both knowingly and unknowingly. Even your greatest heroes are humans. Not every action was meant to hurt you. Maybe they were having a bad day, a bad month, or a horrible year. Not everything that happens to you is about you. I've learned that the best way to make it through this life is to believe the best before you assume the worst, and to give people grace in their moments of weakness.

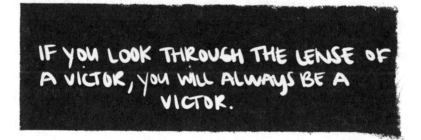

IF YOU LOOK THROUGH THE LENSE OF A VICTOR, YOU WILL ALWAYS BE A VICTOR.

Someone once told me that to make it through the battlefield of relationships, I'd have to just get tougher skin. For a while I tried to do this, but it never seemed to work. It hurts just as bad every time. What happens when my skin gets tough? Does that mean I have no sensitivity toward people anymore? Sadly, I've met a lot of pastors and leaders like that. They love ministry and hate people—sounds like an oxymoron, right? Maybe the offense of people has created a fence in them.

The Bible says an offended person is harder to win back than a fortified city (Prov. 18:19). When I think of a fortified city, I imagine large walls, a gate for entrance and exit, and a safe environment. I think this is the type of environment a person who has been offended is aiming for. We don't call it holding on to offense. We call it protection. When you put up walls, what you thought was keeping people out keeps you locked in. Now, you're watching the gate, being extremely particular about who can come in and go out. The only people you allow in are people who think like you, are angry like you, or are offended the way you've been offended. Together, you build your own little world.

I've noticed something interesting throughout the years. When someone gets offended in my ministry, somewhere along the line, they leave. Then, they become best friends with those who have also been offended in the past, who they may, or may not, have known. Their only bond is offense. What a great plan of the enemy, to bond you with others through what you hate. What then happens, if you choose to forgive, anyone in your circle who is holding more grudges than forgiveness is an unsafe relationship and detrimental to your call. Being a follower of Christ means daily forgiveness. God opposes your toleration and honors confrontation. It's time to stop saying, "We just don't go there with them." Time doesn't heal all wounds—only Jesus does. The Bible is also clear that we all have the opportunity to be offended (Luke 17:1). I have found that many aren't even offended about something that happened to them specifically; they are offended because of someone else's hurt. Offense is like a virus. It spreads by mouth and goes undetected until it's too late. It gets lodged in the heart and controls the flow of what goes in and out. When I started getting tougher skin, I realized that I was doing exactly what those who hurt me did—building my walled city and controlling who came and went. Here's the thing, though. God is not a God of control; He's a God of freedom. He's the one opening the gates, bringing freedom to the captives and sight to the blind.

God spoke to me when I was on this journey, "Jeremy, I don't want you to get tougher skin. I want you to get a tougher source." When people left Jesus, He experienced pain. We see this the most in John 6:67 when He turns to His disciples and asks, "You do not want to leave too, do you?" I can feel His pain because I've been there. I used to believe that the worst pain you could feel was to experience rejection from a father, but I can tell you today that there is no pain as great as being hurt by a son.

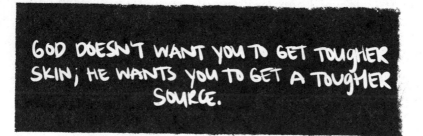

GOD DOESN'T WANT YOU TO GET TOUGHER SKIN; HE WANTS YOU TO GET A TOUGHER SOURCE.

David was a man after God's own heart (Acts 13:22). He didn't have tough skin; he had a tough source. He was rejected on every side, even by his very own father. Take a look at 1 Samuel 16:10–12 with me:

> Jesse had seven of his sons pass before Samuel, but
> Samuel said to him, "The Lord has not chosen these."
> So he asked Jesse, "Are these all the sons you have?"

> *"There is still the youngest," Jesse answered. "He is tending the sheep." Samuel said, "Send for him; we will not sit down until he arrives." So he sent for him and had him brought in. He was glowing with health and had a fine appearance and handsome features. Then the Lord said, "Rise and anoint him; this is the one."*

When Samuel shows up looking to bless the next king of Israel, Jesse, David's dad, calls all his sons in from the field—except for David. Samuel gets to the end of the line of the brothers and asks if there is anyone else. His father is pretty much like, "Well yeah, there's David." Are you kidding me? Rejection from his father is just the beginning of David's troubles.

David is then rejected by his brothers on the battlefield. Goliath taunts the armies of God, and his brothers are soldiers in that army. David shows up with food and inquires about why no one had done anything about the giant. A brother immediately takes a jab at David:

> *When Eliab, David's oldest brother, heard him speaking with the men, he burned with anger at him and asked, "Why have you come down here? And with whom did you leave those few sheep in the wilderness? I know how conceited you are and how wicked your heart is; you came down only to watch the battle"* [1 Samuel 17:28].

Not only does Eliab reject David in his pursuit to advance the Kingdom and follow God, but he puts down David's current position when he says, "With whom did you leave those few sheep?" There will always be people at the wall that were supposed to go past the wall. It was their wall to conquer, but they chose to lie down and make a permanent place out of what was supposed to be a quick stop on the journey. Now, your pursuit to move forward threatens the beliefs they have adopted. We see this in David's brother. The Bible says that his brother burned with anger at David. Eliab was the eldest brother, meaning that because of his position in the family, he was the one that should have been chosen out of the sons of Jesse to be king. But the Lord is not looking for stature or position; He is looking at the heart. Take a look at 1 Samuel 16:6–7:

> *When they arrived, Samuel saw Eliab and thought, "Surely the Lord's anointed stands here before the Lord." But the Lord said to Samuel, "Do not consider his appearance or his height, for I have rejected him. The Lord does not look at the things people look at. People look at the outward appearance, but the Lord looks at the heart."*

Next, David is rejected by his king. Even though David was already anointed to be the next king of Israel, he had to wait many years, running for his life from wicked King Saul. Saul knew that David was God's replacement for him. David was a constant reminder to Saul that he had failed, and God had chosen another. As long as David lived, Saul would have to face this reality. Some Bible scholars believe that David lived in caves for between seven and ten years, surviving on what he could find to eat, never having much time to rest from being pursued by Saul and his army. While living in caves, David gathered what would one day be called the "mighty men." However, they didn't show up to him already mighty. The cave David chose to run to was called Adullam, which means "refuge."

By now, Saul is threatening anyone related to David, including his family in Bethlehem. Saul is full of rage, and David's family members fear for their lives. So, when they hear that David has found a place to hide, they go to join him. David's brothers, sisters, and their children meet up with David at Adullam. His family members weren't the only ones seeking refuge with David. Take a look at 1 Samuel 22:2:

> *All those who were in distress or in debt or discontented gathered around him, and he became their commander. About four hundred men were with him.*

I love this: The distressed, those in debt, and the discontented made him their leader. When I first read this, I couldn't believe it. This was my fearless group. I escaped to the cave, thinking I could heal on my own from past battles. For me, church planting had become my cave where I could start again and deal with my own fears and insecurities. Then, God decided to send people into the cave with me, just as He did with David. My mom, my dad, my two sisters, and their families all moved to help us on this journey. They, too, were running to the cave. Then, my mighty men and mighty women showed up. They didn't show up whole or mighty. Some of them didn't even show up alive in Christ, saved. They showed up on my doorstep broken, distressed, discontent with life. Church leaders showed up not knowing if they could ever live the way they were meant to again. Freedom was no longer a thought in their minds. "Thriving" was not a word in their vocabulary. In fact, "surviving" would better describe them. It's funny how God will send people to you that are stuck in some of the same pits that you're in. He knows that He has put leadership inside you, and when you climb out of the pit you're in, you won't be the only one getting out. Wouldn't it be amazing to know that there was greater purpose to your pain? It changes everything to know that not every pain, every rejection, every hurt you went through was about taking from you; it was about giving to you. It was about giving you a new depth of compassion and connection with those who are in the same pits you have been rescued from.

This is exactly what happened to David. The first group of people God sent were the distressed. The distressed, by definition, are those stuck in a narrow place. Distress could also be described as confinement. To them, the age-old statement "stuck between a rock and a hard place" would ring true. They live with ideas, dreams, and visions of what could be and should be, yet they're locked up without the ability to become. It's those who sit in the graveyard of "should have," "could have," and "would have." The truth of God was choked out by the facts of their lives. There's nothing worse than feeling like you have wasted potential. It's like a bird confined to a cage. This is exactly what it's like to live with untapped potential, which is far greater than the cage you're stuck in.

Some of the mighty men showed up to David's cave distressed; others showed up in debt. If you were in debt too long, your debtor could make you his slave. Not only that, but your family would also be forced to become slaves until your debt was paid off. For Israelites, there was a law in place concerning debt. Every seven years, no matter how great the debt, it was completely forgiven. Those who came to David in debt could have been those who were avoiding the current payments, just waiting for enough time to pass so their debt would be forgiven. They were alive, but not truly able to live. They were waiting for when they could go about their lives without the weight of debt hanging over their shoulders.

Not only did the distressed and those in debt show up to the cave, but the discontented as well. The word *discontented* means "bitter, angry, great, and heavy" in the original Hebrew language. Haven't you noticed that discontentment does exactly this? It causes you to be greatly overwhelmed. You feel heavy because no matter how good things are, it's not enough. It brings a weight to every situation and relationship in your life. It even causes you to give up trying and believing that anything good could happen. When you're discontent, you see everything that doesn't go your way as an attack against you. It robs your ability to see the blessings around you. Your circumstances are not really an attack against you, though; it only feels like an attack because your expectations have not been met.

The cave called Adullam meant "the cave of retreat." It was located only two miles south of the valley of Elah, where David killed Goliath. In the cave, he was with broken men, but standing at a vantage point. He had no forward vision, only the vision to look back at what God had done when he killed the giant. I imagine that he stood on top of this cave many times, staring from afar at the battlefield, where he was once a great warrior surrounded by cheering voices.

Imagine as he stood there with Goliath's sword on his waist. How'd he get the sword? Well, David had previously snuck into the temple and ate some of the sacred bread. The priest who caught him did not get angry with David but protected him instead. He took Goliath's sword, which was hanging in the tabernacle at Nob, and gave it to David as a weapon to protect himself from Saul's advances. Imagine David, staring at the valley, remembering what God had done in his life, now carrying the sword of the giant he had defeated. He must have been filled with thoughts of God's faithfulness. Sometimes, we just need a reminder the devil tried to take us out, but he couldn't do it. He can't do it now, either. The weapons that used to threaten to destroy us have now become weapons at our disposal to defeat the enemy.

The cave of Adullam was known to be covered in olive trees. I find this to be a unique symbol, and I'll tell you why. God placed David in a cave surrounded by olive trees. Olives can be pressed to make olive oil. Olive oil was a valuable commodity in their day, like a currency. It had all kinds of purposes. One of its uses was fuel for lamps. It was also used to make anointing oil, hair and body products, to heal wounds and bruises, and of course, as a cooking agent. There was a process for making olive oil. First, the olives had to be plucked. Next, they had to be trotted upon and crushed, until what was sour became fragrant. To get the oil, both the fruit and its seed had to be completely crushed. The forms of crushing they used were trotting underfoot or a press, which was a giant stone that was rolled over the fruit repeatedly. Before it's crushed, all you will taste is bitterness. It's the great weight of the press and the heaviness of the trotting that removes the bitterness and produces the oil. The olive's value is only realized after the crushing.

God is trying to give you fresh oil. The crushing of yesterday won't be enough for the power you need tomorrow. The crushing David had been through was enough to kill the giant, but in order to become king, he had to be crushed again. Jesus, too, was crushed and trotted upon. He took the weight of sin so He could become the power of God in our lives. The cave was training

David to lead a nation. This place of great pain became his turning point personally and the turning point for nations. It was in the cave that he learned how to worship and how to war. He learned to lead hundreds, which prepared him to lead thousands.

No, David would not become king in a palace; he would become king in a cave. God was cutting the "Saul" out of David—the insecurity, or should I say, the security found in man. God alone was going to be David's hiding place. God was going to use David's pain to connect him to his future army. Imagine the powerful connection formed between a king and his people after he steps off his throne and goes through the same suffering of those he leads. You cannot help someone get to where they're going if you don't understand where they've been.

Everyone has an opinion, and everyone believes their opinion is right. Typically, we choose to listen to those who have walked in our shoes and understand us. Yes, I believe that we should all be free to have opinions, but not all opinions are necessary to share, and not all are valid. My opinion is only as valid as my experience. Many people have strong opinions about things they've never done themselves or have never experienced. I have found that some of the decisions others made that I didn't understand made more sense to me as I walked in their shoes. For instance, my dad was an incredible dad, but I can still find things I wish he would've done growing up. Yet, when I became a dad, the grace I have toward him grew because I realized how much grace I need as a dad. Unless we've walked in the shoes of the person we're critiquing, our opinion is simply that—an opinion. It has not been tested or proved true.

Here is David, given a chance to walk in the shoes of those he would lead, and together they were transformed in the cave.

Those who were in distress, in debt, or discontent became known as David's mighty men. Then, just when David starts getting comfortable in the cave, a prophet shows up and speaks this word in 1 Samuel 22:5:

> But the prophet Gad said to David, "Do not stay in the stronghold. Go into the land of Judah." So David left and went to the forest of Hereth.

The prophet was telling David, "Don't die in the cave. The cave was never meant to be your home. It was only for a season." The prophet tells David to step out of the cave and go back to the land of Judah. The word *Judah* strikes a chord in me because in Hebrew, *Judah* means "praise." Judah was Leah's fourth son with Jacob. She named her son Judah because she praised God because of his birth, saying, "This time I will praise the Lord" (Gen. 29:35). Judah became one of the twelve tribes of Israel, and this is the very lineage that David came from. To me, when God tells David to come out of the cave and step into Judah, I believe God was calling him and his mighty men into worship. Or even greater, He was calling them back to their roots, the root of praise. At this point, Saul was still pursuing David, yet God called him out of the cave and into the forest. The forest was symbolic of unfruitfulness. It was not a place where things grew as a result of man's work. It was the wild; things still grew there, but they grew without anyone tending to them. It's almost as if God was saying, "David, I'm going to take you into the middle of the wild, and I will be your cave. I will be your protection." We can see this in many of David's psalms. He said things like, "The Lord is my rock, my fortress and my deliverer; my God is my rock...my salvation, my stronghold" (Ps. 18:2). God was teaching David that He would indeed give him a physical cave, but at the end of the day, the Lord was the only cave needed. The posture of true praise is acknowledging that God is our rock. Isn't it unique that this forest was still in Judah? An unfamiliar and uncomfortable place was still a place named "praise."

God being David's cave of protection reminds me of the type of power that God wants to release on the Church. After Jesus rose from the dead, He was talking with His disciples. He had shown many signs and given proof that it was indeed Him, and then He instructed them to stay in the city until they had been clothed with power (Luke 24:49). He referred to the Holy Spirit's power as if it were an article of clothing. I used to believe this was something that you put on, like a person would put on a shirt or some pants. In this Scripture, though, the phrase "clothed with power" is the Greek word *endyō*, which means "to sink into." "To sink into" is different from "to put on." When you put something on, it is in your power to choose to wear, or not to wear, that item of clothing. You decide and you control. When you sink into something, the item does not shift or change. It is you who must mold to its form and will. The very essence of it not moving gives it its power. The power of God that He has for us is not something we put on; it is something we hide in. This is the same as the picture that I get with David. It was as if the cave was a physical representation of what God was going to do—protect and hide David. If David trusted further, he could hide in the strength of God alone. His enemies would change, but his mindset and understanding would be renewed to know that no matter what he walked through, his God would protect him.

At the very core of our beings, God built in us the need to hide in something. For example, when Adam heard God's voice in the garden, what was the first thing he did? He hid. The problem wasn't that he hid; the problem was that he hid in the wrong thing. When you hide in God's presence, you won't feel shame, even when you're naked. The moment he hid behind creation, though, shame came from his nakedness.

Next, we have Peter, who denied Christ, then hid in the shadows, following at a distance. He was fearful and intimidated, and eventually, he went back to hiding in what he knew all of his life—fishing. On the day of Pentecost, we see a different Peter—bold, courageous, filled with compassion and faith. I don't believe that Peter stopped hiding that day. He just changed who he hid in.

David needed protection, not only from his father and brothers, but also from the king and his army. Even the mighty men would one day turn on David. His very own wife, Michal, rejected him when she peered out her window and judged David for dancing before the Lord in a way that made her uncomfortable. The last and final straw was when David's own son led a rebellion against him. If David was going to make it through all of the rejection and danger, he was going to need to hide in God. However, God allowed the rejection. He could have stopped it, but it was an important tool in the Master's hand, refining him on his journey to becoming a man after God's own heart.

Be encouraged today if you face rejection on all sides. James 1:2–4 says:

> *Consider it pure joy, my brothers and sisters, whenever*
> *you face trials of many kinds, because you know that*

> *the testing of your faith produces perseverance. Let*
> *perseverance finish its work so that you may be mature*
> *and complete, not lacking anything.*

You might as well praise through your pain, dance through your drought, and worship with your wounds because the Lord who called you will use the rejection you've experienced to push you closer to your destiny. God is the one who sets you apart, making it impossible to fit in. David says it like this in Psalm 4:3:

> *Know that the Lord has set apart his faithful servant for*
> *himself; the Lord hears when I call to him.*

God had to make it so you didn't fit, in because those who fit in don't seek for where they really fit—in Him. Every hero of faith was rejected, including God's Son, Jesus. He definitely didn't fit in. Rejection can't stop you, though. It's the view you have of rejection that can take the biggest toll on your life.

I always believed Jesus had tough skin, but the more I read about Him, the more I discover that He was just like me. Every one rejected this guy, but it was hard for me to grasp. Everything I knew was the opposite of this. Jesus was this blue-eyed, brown-haired man with a white robe and blue sash. He had the perfect body, handsome features, and was loved by His peers and His family, right? This is how Hollywood and the Church have portrayed Him in movies and Easter productions, so that's how I saw Him. Jesus has always been displayed as perfect, or at least that's how I saw Him. This was until I read the Bible with my lenses of "church culture" off and came across this verse:

> *He was despised and rejected by men, a man of*
> *suffering and familiar with pain. Like one from whom*

people hide their faces he was despised, and we held him in low esteem. Surely he took up our pain and bore our suffering, yet we considered him punished by God, stricken by him, and afflicted [Isaiah 53:3–4].

This is a different portrayal of Jesus than the Americanized one I saw in my mind. He experienced the pain of rejection, the sorrow, the suffering. Although I am comforted by the truth that He can relate to my pain, it doesn't change the fact that planting a church has turned out to be the hardest thing I have ever stepped into. It feels like how one day the crowds cried out "Hosanna!" to Jesus, and the next day, the same people cried out "Crucify Him!" Some of the very people who came and loved me, have been the very people who left because they couldn't stand me.

For the last few years, we have had tons of fun—new faces, new decisions for Christ, and new family. Do you know what comes with people, though? Hurt and pain. I have had to learn how to not harden my heart when it comes to people who promise a lot and leave before the promise is fulfilled. To forgive those who abandon ship when the first storm comes. I choose to love those who sabotage the ship's mission altogether. I have had the option to either run from people or to get a strong mind and a soft heart. Not a hard heart and a soft mind. Again, when I took the advice of getting tougher skin to walk out my call in loving people, I became distant from the very people I needed to be close to to reach. Most leaders have chosen to do this very thing because the call can be tough; this ultimately renders them ineffective. As I read more about Jesus, I saw through the pages that He never got tough skin; He had emotions and was hurt by others at times, saddened by their choice to leave, and felt the full weight of their hurt. So I asked Him how He did it, how to never stop loving people. He said, "Jeremy, I didn't get tougher skin; I tapped into a stronger source."

Choose the same and you'll not only service the call, you'll thrive. I have chosen again and again when rejection comes to toughen my source, not toughen my skin. Only by getting a tough source, which is God the Father, not tough skin, will we make it. The Father is the one who helps us walk continually in the practice of forgiveness and at the same time not abandon the call. Through forgiveness God gives you new eyes on everything, including yourself. Rejection will always be there, but its power breaks when you see how God accepts you. Identity as sons and daughters empowers us to embrace the call. Romans 8:31 rings true: "What, then, shall we say in response to these things? If God is for us, who can be against us?" The answer is simple: no one, no fear, no depression, no rejection, no one! It's the rejection of man that drives us to Him.

> *Large crowds were traveling with Jesus, and turning to them he said: "If anyone comes to me and does not hate his father and mother, his wife and children, his brothers and sisters—yes, even his own life—he cannot be my disciple. And anyone who does not carry his cross and follow me cannot be my disciple" (Luke 14:25–27).*

NOT ALL GROWTH IS GOOD GROWTH

If there's anything I've learned along the journey, it is that not all growth is good growth. Cancer grows just like a muscle does, but there is no one in their right mind who wakes up in the morning and longs for that type of growth. Whether planting a church or building an organization of any size, we celebrate growth. We are discouraged by downsizing. In other words, we love when they come in and hate when they leave. Love to hire and hate to fire. During my time pastoring a church, I have found that it seems like people come just to leave. Sometimes it feels like it's just a matter of time before their tune changes from, "We love you!" to "We can't stand you," and soon you notice on their Instagram feed that they're posting about their new favorite pastor or church. Being transparent, this is probably the hardest thing I've had to walk through as a pastor. It's always exciting when people come. My wife and I are buzzing all night long about all the visitors that show up and how we could see them fitting into the plan that God has here in LA.

It is so encouraging to look at numbers and see growth, but it would be foolish to think that God is always in the growth. In fact, I have found He is just as much into subtraction as He is into addition. He is into division as much as He is into multiplication. Jesus was constantly trying to thin out the crowd. He was constantly trying to check the hearts of those who followed. If I was church planting with Jesus, I probably would have taken the mic away and said, "You can't say that, Jesus. Tell them they're loved. Tell them they're beautiful. Don't say all the stuff You've been saying." At the worst times, just when they had built up the crowd, Jesus would say offensive, radical things. They started giving to the mission, and then Jesus would get up there and say something that would offend them again, and of course, not explain it. People would walk away and say things like, "That's just too hard. We can't follow that."

One time Jesus got up at the end of His sermon and said, "Unless you eat the flesh of the Son of Man and drink his blood, you have no life in you" (John 6:53). To this Jewish audience who believed that blood and flesh were considered unclean and a defilement to even be in contact with, this would have been the most offensive thing Jesus could have uttered. He knew the beliefs and customs of His audience. He was Jewish! So why did He do it? Was He crazy? Did He just want to be hard-headed? No. It's because He was separating those who were following a vision from those who were following a man with a vision. When it came to the people who were following a vision, as soon as the vision wasn't playing to their advantage, they were moving on. These people would leave by the thousands. As soon as Jesus shared that the vision was to die, there were people who said, "Well then, I guess this is where we part ways," and they looked for the next person's vision to follow.

The problem with getting really excited when people come is that we tend to look for what we are doing right; when they leave, we look for what we did wrong. Could it be that you were doing it right when they came and when they left? Could it be that God is protecting you when they leave? Like a surgeon removing a tumor or a limb with gangrene, it's never fun, but if it remains in the body, what looks like growth will become your demise. I want to be clear. I'm not likening people to a tumor or a disease, but sometimes the attitudes and spirits they carry are. I also am not advocating that we should have small churches, and that big churches are bad in any way, or that your company or dream should remain small. I think our churches will have to grow to reach our lost cities. Our companies will need to take more ground and hire more people to change the world. However, we want the growth to be in disciples, not just growth in numbers. Moses's generation followed a vision of a better life when Moses asked who wanted to go to the land with milk and honey. Everyone and their mom wanted to go. A leader will never have a problem getting people to go out of their Egypt or their place of suffering. The difficulty is usually found in getting them into their promised land. In order to get someone into their promise, there will be moments they will need to continue to follow when they can't see. To be honest, sometimes the leader can't even see. The hope is that the leader can see God, and God always sees and leads the leader.

Joshua's generation followed a man with a vision. It was a family (literally) pushing the enemy out of their land. We see this with the first miraculous moment after they crossed the Jordan River. God told Joshua not to ram the wall down, but to instead shout it down. He instructed Joshua that before they were to shout, they were to march around the city for seven days. During this time, the people of the city were mocking God's plan as it unfolded. What faith those marching would have had to have to willingly march in circles and remain steadfast while being ridiculed from the wall.

God rarely calls us as leaders to do something that makes sense in the natural. So because of this, some people won't be able to continue forward. If we look at the picture of Jesus, we see that His call was so extreme that very few disciples made it to the cross. If you're reading this and you're a leader, you must be ready for people to leave as much as you're ready for them to come. Both come with the territory. However, this does not make it easy. It has always been tough for me when people move on. I'm not sure it will ever get easy.

Too Many Companions

> *A man of many companions may come to ruin, but there is a friend who sticks closer than a brother* (Proverbs 18:24 ESV).

A companion is someone who is on the journey with you, but not necessarily on the journey for you. There are two different types of companions, the first is an opportunist. Their attraction is the mission. The focus isn't so much who they are on the mission with, but the mission itself. These people fall in love with the vision of the person. It resonates and lines up with where they see themselves. If you're going to the same place, what an opportunity for them to join the journey! They believe you'll get them where they want to go faster so they join the stream of the vision. An opportunist isn't necessarily bad to have on the team, but you have to know why they are with you. They will stay with you as long as you are getting them closer to the place they are heading. However, you must keep in mind that opportunists will leap out of your life the moment they find a faster route to where they are going. There will be emotional promises made that will never be kept because the most important thing is the end goal, even beyond keeping their word. One week, you're the greatest thing in their life, and the next week, it's something or someone else. Just know when they leave you, their time in your life is done. They may be a part of your history but are not a part of your destiny.

There is no one in my life who isn't there on purpose. Although people will have agendas behind why they walk with you, God has your back. It is God who gives and God who takes away. Don't be shocked when an opportunist leaves you; let them go. They were never with you in the first place. They may talk big about you, but it's not you, it's your vision they are following. They were focused on the cause, and if there is another way to further their agenda, they will leave you in a heartbeat. Prepare yourself. If you thought they were a friend, if you thought they loved you, you will have your heart broken. They never loved you, they loved where you could take them. You were their emotional or spiritual Uber driver. Don't get it twisted thinking you're in a car with friends going to your favorite spot. No, you are just a means to an end. They are kind on the ride, but whether you're going to be around or not after you get them to their destination is of no value to them. I know this sounds harsh, but it is the reality of what Solomon was saying in Proverbs, that many come to ruin because they have too many companions. Companions will come and go.

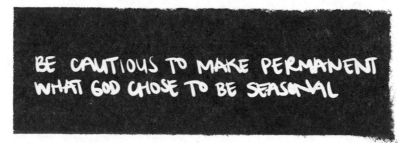

BE CAUTIOUS TO MAKE PERMANENT WHAT GOD CHOSE TO BE SEASONAL

We live in downtown LA, and buildings are remodeled quite often here. While they are being remodeled, scaffolding can be seen and coverings are placed on the outside of the buildings as they are under construction. The scaffolding goes up directly against a building. Most of the time, you can't see where the scaffolding ends and the building starts. It's placed so tightly against the building that they look one in the same. The scaffolding doesn't stay up forever, though. When the building is finished, the same workers who put up the scaffolding take it down. It is then that the true beauty comes forth from the work that was going on behind the scaffolding. As God removes the scaffolding in your life, don't let it mess with your peace. You may feel like you lost out, but you didn't; you gained. When the scaffolding comes down, the building is revealed. There are some people who God sends into your life to help get you to your next destination. They didn't come to stay; they came to leave. God's purpose for them was seasonal in your life. Be cautious to make permanent what God chose to be seasonal. You have to love them when they come and love them when they go, and know that the Lord gives and the Lord takes away. Don't let your heart get bitter over opportunists.

I like to call the second category of companions "freedom fighters." These are the people who are in it for what you're against. This group rallies around what they dislike or hate. They have found enough common hate for something that they build a companionship from it. These can be great companions when you're in a battle because, as long as there is a fight, they are in the trenches with you. However, many forget that these people are fighters. Don't let it take you by surprise when the fight turns against you. They are fighters at heart and feel a rush in the fight. They were never really for you; they were just against what you were against. We can see this in people who get offended at a situation or a person. They can rally quickly and form fast new companionships based on what they hate. The fuel for the fire isn't what they love as much as what they hate. They find camaraderie in what they are angry at. In a way, they carry one another's anger and protect one another's offense. Thank God there is a friend who sticks closer than a brother (Prov. 18:24). The people who have left you have only revealed to you what relationships you should place true value on. They showed you that you need to really value those who aren't for what you're for or against what you're against, but those who are simply for you. This is why we don't just follow a vision; we follow a leader with a vision. Paul didn't say, "Follow my vision." He said, "Be imitators of me, as I am of Christ" the person, Paul (1 Cor. 11:1 ESV). Every person has walked through the pain of people leaving, even Jesus. Today, allow His process of subtraction, or better yet, welcome it as you would welcome His addition.

THE PLANTED
LIFE

THE PLANTED LIFE

8
CHAPTER

How foolish! What you sow does not come to life unless it dies *[1 Corinthians 15:36]*.

God's ultimate purpose for the seed is not death but life. The seed is not just buried, it's planted. God allows the burrying process because its the only way to produce fruit we can call this resurrection life.

It's like a package of seeds. There's a picture on the package of what the end product should look like. On the package of you, there is a picture of God's call on your life. Maybe like me, for the first part of your life, you were so excited about the vision, so you went around showing people the vision that was on the outside of the package. God spoke to you, and it was so shocking and so amazing that you instantly found identity and purpose in the picture. Many times people make the picture their idol because they're embarrassed about the smallness of the seed.

We are often consumed with the picture and forget about the process. God is finished with the picture and invested in the process. The more we look in the mirror, the more we feel like the picture looks nothing like the seed. The problem is when we don't honor the process, we ultimately don't honor the seed. We show the picture, but since the seed looks nothing like the picture we honor the picture and are embarrassed of the seed. God gives vision, then He immediately opens the package, reaches His hand inside, and pulls out the seed. Now out of the package, the picture is gone, and we look nothing like what we're believing for. What we fail to recognize is that the seed is the picture, but first it has to die. The seed has no beauty. The seed isn't something I want to show anyone. This is where it starts to get real. That's why we need a community of faith around, not fear. This is where it starts to get real in relationships. Where we don't just talk about where we're going; we talk about where we currently are. We lose the power of the seed when we are afraid of the process the seed must go through. We know that God has power; we know that God has a purpose; but do you trust He also has a plan?

Many people live their whole lives depressed about the seed, yet the seed is the picture in its embryonic stage. It's just a matter of having enough vision to believe in the process of the seed. The watermelon seed is a watermelon in its immature state. Stop there for a moment and ask yourself: Can I believe in the God vision about people's lives while they are in their immature state? I believe that true maturity is the ability to look at the immature state of what God is creating in someone's life and honor that. If we never honor the seed, we will never see what the seed could become. How many apples are in the seed? How many trees are in the apple? How many orchards are in the tree? The answer is unlimited, but it all starts with the hand on the seed. Submission to the process determines the progress. Remember, God is the gardener. He sees the power in the seed even if the seed can't see it. He's not threatened by the fact that the seed is not yet full grown because He knows that it is just a matter of time. He takes the seed out of the package. Then He takes the seed to the middle of the field alone. There are moments on this journey of faith that I've had to walk alone. What I failed to recognize is that sometimes the darkness surrounding me is His hand holding me. The isolation wasn't rejection; it was Him choosing me. From this point, the farmer digs a hole in the middle of a field. The farmer (God), not satan, drops you into the hole. Some of us may be cursing the very pit we were called to. The grime and dirt and manure begins to surround you, and it feels like being buried, but you have actually been planted. The act of burial is something that people do when something is dead and not ever coming back. When you're planted, there is something deep inside waiting to be unlocked. You are planted, not buried.

SOMETIMES THE DARKNESS SURROUNDING ME IS HIS HAND HOLDING ME.

> *The righteous will flourish like a palm tree, they will grow like a cedar of Lebanon; planted in the house of the Lord, they will flourish in the courts of our God. They will still bear fruit in old age, they will stay fresh and green* (Psalm 92:12–14).

See, today I believe that many who think they are planted are actually potted. Psalm 92 does not promise that the potted will flourish; it promises that the planted will flourish. What's the difference? Potted believers are like a nomadic tribe that moves from this congregation to the next, this tribe to the next. They don't choose one church to go to; they divide their time between multiple. Just like young adults go clubbing, many Christian young adults go "churching." At first, this seems fun, but it doesn't allow for deep roots and long-lasting discipleship. In order for roots to grow, it takes time in the same soil without the limitations of the pot. Some people are potted because they don't know any different, while others who used to be planted chose to uproot themselves from the garden for various reasons. If you've been planted in God's house for long, you realize it's not always easy to remain. Out of your pot and into the soil of God's garden, you're right next to others. It's as if you're out in the open, subject to the elements, where there seems to be no protection. At least in the plastic pot, you know where your walls are. It may keep you in, but it also keeps others out.

The thinking of the potted believer is, "I need my pot so no one else can hurt me." We have allowed the enemy to trick us into settling for a dwarfed life of safety at the expense of a flourishing life of growth. This is the difference between a fearful life and the abundant fearless life that God desires for us to have. The enemy knows when your roots are held back by your walls, you will have limited resources, limited potential, and your growth will be stifled. What if this pot is smaller than the destiny of your roots? Your roots were designed to withstand the wild and produce much fruit. Your destiny will not be unlocked through safety; it will be unlocked through courage. It was for this reason that Jesus was not murdered in a cathedral between two candles; He was killed at a place called Golgotha, which means the Place of the Skull, where sinners mocked, soldiers gambled, and disciples ran. The region was so multicultural that His title was written in three different languages. Jesus was out with the sinners because He works best where hurting people are.

The fruit of the Spirit is best tasted where people are starving. God begins to produce fruit in your life, but not fruit meant to display, fruit to be eaten. Jesus said He wants to produce fruit that will last, not because the fruit will last forever. That would be plastic fruit. The point is that fruit would remain on your branches;

as soon as one piece of fruit is pulled off, the next piece of fruit is already growing. In and out of season, there would be growth.

> WE HAVE ALLOWED THE ENEMY TO TRICK US INTO SETTLING FOR A DWARFED LIFE OF SAFETY AT THE EXPENSE OF A FLOURISHING LIFE OF GROWTH.

I'll never forget when I went to Colombia to preach at a youth conference. What an honor and what an amazing movement happening! We were sitting down with the pastors and eating together. Their favorite thing to do was to take me to experience their amazing food. They took great pride in introducing me to the different flavors of Colombia. They began to bring fruit to me that I'd never seen. He told me that they had around 26 fruits that aren't found anywhere else in the world. This is because Colombia doesn't have multiple seasons; it has only one. It's the season of growth. It is because they live so close to the equator that they don't go through winter like the rest of the world does. They're always in the season of harvest, and because of that, when you put something in the ground, things are instantly produced. The Church needs to be a Church that is living in one season, since we are so close to Jesus. I wonder what fruit has been stifled in our lives because we keep potting ourselves instead of planting ourselves next to where Jesus is. People say the Church is not where Jesus is. Yes it is; it's His bride. Church is not where Jesus is? He describes Himself as the head of His body, and the body is His Church. One thing I've learned about potted Christians is you look nice in the pot, but as soon as you get in a storm, you're in trouble. The storm blows the pot around and leaves the plant destroyed because it has beauty but no stability. In contrast, if you've been planted, the storm will test you but not destroy you.

Recently, I had a great conversation with one of my friends about church. I explained to him that some of our young adults are broke and some actually own businesses. Some say you can't build a church on young adults because they don't have the time and the resources to fuel a church. Also most young adults are very transient because they have nothing that forces them to plant. When you have a family, you're stuck in school districts, and you buy a house so your kids will be able to grow up in it. It's a bad thing to move when you're a family, but when you're a young adult, you're transient—you're on the move. When you're a young adult, there is nothing to hold you down in one place. In fact, everything is trying to draw you out.

I began to ask God, "Why would You give me a church of all young adults when they can be transient?" I noticed this in our leadership. We had raised up over 200 leaders at this point, and 100 of them had moved on. Some could not afford to stay in LA, so they just left; some got sidetracked with their businesses or dreams. It was like every time I'd talk to them, they'd say, "I have to go now," "I have to move now," "I have to do this now." I started getting discouraged thinking, "God, why did You give me a church with such transient people, yet tell me to build a church out of this?" I began to pray and ask God to tell me what to do. He began to speak to me and said, "The church is the soil that they are to plant in." The love of Jesus is unconditional. Once you get planted in the church, you can find out very fast if it's the love of Jesus inside of you or just the love of a better life. The love of Jesus will stay up longer than you want to and do more for people than you'd be willing to typically do. The love of Jesus works best when it's planted in the manure and in the fields of other people's lives. I noticed a trend, that we have a hard time loving each other inside the Church, but we love the people outside the Church easily. According to Scripture, they are dead and have no love to offer you, so why does it feel like this? I think sometimes it feels easier with them because we aren't expecting anything from them. From people in the Church, we expect so much more. We get offended to the level that someone lets our expectations down. We weren't let down by them, just our expectations of them.

In the early days of Fearless, God spoke to me and showed me that Fearless Church is to be the soil that helps them get rooted. When they plant themselves in the house and don't just stay in pots, something begins to shift in their lives. The Bible promises us that they'll produce fruit and stay green. So I begin to teach that at church and began to see people hashtag #plantedinthehouse on social media. When the storms come, our roots have already attached to something that doesn't move, so the storm no longer destroys us, but only helps us. It helps us hold the fruit that we've been developing so that the world can experience the fruit of Jesus in our lives. It's only in the storm. We're walking through hell and high water, and we still have a smile on our faces because our source is beneath the surface. Our source is greater than what you can see. Our source is drawing from things from another world. God designed the fertile ground of the Church to be soil that we plant our lives in.

Instead, we often stay in our pots, never getting the nutrients we truly need, so our growth is limited. Our fruit is dwarfed and our impact stifled by the next storm. We are only joyful on sunny days and miss the true power of being planted. Our pots keep others out. It works for a season, but pretty soon you realize you're in a community divided, you're in a crowd, but lonely, and your source is limited. God is an unlimited God. He is a river underneath the surface that He wants you to tap into. It will not happen as long as you remain in the pot. Today is a day to get planted in the house. Being planted means that you have to go unnoticed, unseen, and there may be years that no one, including you, remembers the picture that you saw on the seed package. There may be years that you forget about the picture. You forget the reason you're even planted. But eventually something starts growing. It doesn't even look like the old you. I have found that when I finally hold the promise of lasting fruit, it's like I'm experiencing the joy of the picture all over again. I've been deeply planted for so long that at times, the planting felt like a burial. But I had to remind myself that after death there is resurrection. Choose to let go of your fear of the planted life by looking to Christ who planted Himself right in the middle of the manure of man. After the first storm, you'll be glad you did. I've learned many times I needed my community as much as they needed me. If we keep our eyes on pain, we'll never plant. We will miss the fruit He locked inside of us on the other side of the storm. You were chosen not to be potted and temporary but to be planted and permanent, bearing much fruit.

> *You did not choose Me but I chose you, and appointed you that you would go and bear fruit, and that your fruit would remain, so that whatever you ask of the Father in My name He may give to you* [John 15:16 NASB].

FOR I AM CONVINCED THAT NEITHER DEATH NOR LIFE, NEITHER ANGELS NOR DEMONS, NEITHER THE PRESENT NOR THE FUTURE, NOR ANY POWERS, NEITHER HEIGHT NOR DEPTH, NOR ANYTHING ELSE IN ALL CREATION, WILL BE ABLE TO SEPARATE US FROM THE LOVE OF GOD THAT IS IN CHRIST JESUS OUR LORD.

ROMANS 8:38

PRAYER– THE KEY TO THE KINGDOM

PRAYER-
THE KEY
TO THE
KINGS

CHAPTER

9

107

You are the light of the world. A town built on a
hill cannot be hidden. Neither do people light a
lamp and put it under a bowl. Instead they put it
on its stand, and it gives light to everyone in the
house. In the same way, let your light shine before
others, that they may see your good deeds and
glorify your Father in heaven [Matthew 5:14–16].

In Matthew we were instructed to put the lamp
on a lampstand. We aren't to worship or crave the lampstand.
No, we are to crave the light. We need the light. We can get
so caught up in the lampstand, which is simply the thing that
showcases the light, that we start worshiping the lampstand.
The problem with making the lampstand the big thing is that
it brings no light to the house. Your talent and your platform
are just the stand that the light goes on. What people need is
not one more performance, one more song, one more sermon,
or one more book. What they need is for the light to be placed
back on the stand to bring light to the entire house.

I learned this firsthand. My lampstand was the gift of creativity.
I had done everything and then some. I tried every creative
idea that my young mind could think of, yet all had failed. What
I saw with my heart, and what I saw with my eyes were two different
things. The journey of a pioneer, while it sounds romantic,
is daunting. It's full of upsets and frustrations as you trek on
the road less traveled, or maybe even the one never traveled. If
you can relate, hang in there. Keep moving forward. You're not
alone. I have hit many walls along this journey, and I'm sure I
will hit many more. I have now found that it's who you listen to
at the wall that determines if you settle there or press on.

I hit a wall. It wasn't the first time in ministry, but this time was different. I'll never forget walking out to speak that night. I was ready to close worship, and as I looked at the crowd, I was disheartened. The room was filled with empty seats. and although a few leaders at the front of the stage were giving all their praise to God, the rest of the crowd looked uninterested, bored, or focused on something outside the room. I walked right back off the stage and went into my office. I burst into tears, full of anger and frustration. I had done everything I could imagine, yet I couldn't grow this ministry. I longed to set it on fire like I'd seen in my dreams. Maybe I just wasn't the guy. Maybe God got mixed up. I fell to my knees in my office and heard the drums beating through my wall. It felt as though I was beating on God's chest. It took a minute, and then I heard God say as clear as day, "Are you done yet?" I cried out, "God, I am so done! I have nothing left. I can't do this." Then God said, "Good, this was the place I wanted you. Are you sure you're done with all your big ideas, all your catchy phrases, all your clever sermons, all the ways it will work for you?" I screamed out, "God, I'm so done!" "Good," He said. "Now I can begin. The first thing I want you to do is rip up your sermon. It's not yours anyways." He was right. I had gotten it online from one of my favorite preachers. I ripped up my sermon, and then God said, "When you go out to the mic, I'll tell you what to say." *Well, this should be interesting,* I thought.

I walked back onto the stage with nothing in my mind to say. Sure enough when I grabbed the mic, words began to come out. The first thing God had me do was ask everyone who was sick in the room to come to the stage. After I said it, I thought, *No big deal. This is youth ministry. There won't be a bunch of sick kids.* Boy, was I wrong. The whole stage was packed with kids I'd never seen before—one guy in a wheelchair, three with crutches, others just holding up a part that was in pain. I thought, *Oh great. I didn't know God was going to put me on the spot like this.* However, the tables were turned, and He was challenging my faith to put Him on the spot. With my shallow faith, I turned to the first person. Good thing all it takes is a mustard seed to move mountains. With that, I began to pray. Never before and never since have I experienced something so supernatural. One by one, the teenagers began to get healed. As I prayed, the first guy just began yelling that his leg was hot. Instantly, I realized it was working. Sure enough, the miracle power of God was in the room. Every student on that stage was healed that night except for one, who I still pray for to this day.

Over 30 visible miracles took place that night. The whole room was on the edge of their seats. This was no longer business as usual. The Lord was doing miracles in our midst. The Bible came alive that night, and this one-dimensional Jesus became 3D. At the end of the night, I finished with a salvation call. There was no one in the room who didn't want Jesus. That night we had church like the first church, full of life and celebration because the students had met a real Jesus.

As I walked off the stage, I heard God speak to me again. "Did you like that?" "Did I like that? That was incredible. I feel alive again." "Good. I'm now in charge of your youth ministry. This week, instead of working, I want you to pray. You're a workaholic so that should be a lot." I thought, *Are you kidding me, God?* The bad news was He heard my thoughts and responded with "no, I'm not kidding. For 8 hours a day, some days 10, I want you to come into your office, shut the door, and cry out to Me."

I said, "God, how will I do that? They pay me to be the youth pastor here. What if someone finds out?" "You mean you'll get in trouble spending time with Me?" "That's not what I mean, God. What if someone wants a meeting with me? What if there's a student leader or parent that needs counseling?" Then God said, "If anyone needs a meeting, ask them before the meeting, 'Will you pray with me for an hour? If God answers your prayer during that time, then let's cancel the meeting.'" Funny thing was that this did happen. However, every time, within thirty minutes the person would walk out of the room. Either they got their need met or they were tired of praying. Either way, it was much better. I don't really like meetings anyway.

So, the next morning I walked into my office, turned on some music, and did exactly as God said. I'm not sure I had ever prayed that long in my life. About two hours in, I ran out of songs and requests, but that's when the Holy Spirit began to minister to me in ways I cannot describe. It was almost as if He was doing delicate surgery on my heart. He began to heal every hurt, every fear, and every offense. I found myself repenting, forgiving, and being forgiven. One hour I was bawling my eyes out, the next I was rejoicing. Sometimes I just sat in silence. For the first time in my life, I was okay with silence. Typically, in the silence my mind would wander to all the things I had to do, but in these moments, God was giving me a new rest. The next day I did the same thing. No one asked about it, so I didn't tell anyone. The day after, I did the same thing. By the time Wednesday of the next week rolled around, I didn't have a sermon. That was okay with me, though, because the week before I didn't seem to need one. I couldn't wait for service to start. There was a new excitement in the air. The room was a little fuller than the week before. People were actually inviting their friends! It became a place where we expected God to show up and do miracles. It's funny how that works. It's so much better than flyers and social media campaigns.

I didn't study to give a message that night, but as I opened my Bible, the words came alive. When it was time to close the message. everyone had their heads bowed and eyes closed. Abruptly, a young man got up from the middle of the crowd and started making his way toward the front of the stage. I thought, *This is interesting. People are answering the altar call before I give it.* He was not answering any kind of call from my message or the Jesus I preached. As the young man got closer, he looked up at me, and no joke, out of his face jumped the most demonic face I'd ever seen. It was like something out of a scary dream or a horror movie. Then the young man turned from me with an evil smirk and went back into the crowd. On his way out, he walked halfway down the aisle and grabbed a young lady out of her seat. He then violently attempted to drag her out of the room. You could tell by her face that she had no clue who this guy was or why he was pulling her out of the room. As she screamed hysterically, everyone in the room was frozen. No one tried to stop him. I closed my eyes and began to pray in the Spirit, and within seconds the young man let go of the girl and was at my feet. I was not sure how he got there so fast, but I didn't care. He begged me to "stop praying like that." You better believe I kept praying like that! In fact, I started praying louder, and this time, into the mic. The young man began to scream, and I put my hand on his forehead. What happened next was something out of a science-fiction movie. He was on his knees and dramatically flipped and slammed onto his back. I'm not kidding. He began to squirm around on the floor like a snake.

The whole room was silent as this battle between the preacher and demon-possessed student took place. No one moved. All eyes were focused on the young man and what I would do next. Then I heard a voice as clear as day say, "The enemy is trying to rob Me of My glory. He's pulling the attention off of what I was about to do, to his agenda, fear. Don't cast out this demon here. Send the boy to the back room." I was relieved. I grabbed the first leader I could find. You should've seen his eyes when I told him, "Alright, you're up. Take him to the back room and cast this devil out of him." As soon as the young man was dragged out by a few leaders, the room remained in a stunned hush. I then shared with the students what God had just told me and that He wanted to bring breakthrough to their lives. I reminded them that the battle between light and darkness is real and that the enemy did not want them to be free. I continued by telling them that the power of God is greater than any enemy that would walk into the room. That night, everyone got saved all over again. We ended on a high, and by the time we were done, the kid who had been squirming all over the floor was sitting upright in my office, not knowing what had happened. We led him in some further prayer for deliverance from alcohol and drugs, and then we led him in the sinner's prayer. That night his life changed forever. Then I heard God say, "Did you like that?" I said, "No I didn't, but I did like that You were with me." Then God said, "I want you to pray another week."

The next day, I came in and began to pray; about two hours in, I noticed it was darker outside my office than usual. I looked out of my window through my blinds, and I saw the lights in my secretary's office were off as well, and I heard music coming from her cubicle. I peeked out of my door to find that my secretary was praying as well. I guess I couldn't get mad at her for not working, so I left her alone. About midday, two more leaders had gathered with her, and by the end of the day, there were 10 people in the room crying out to God. The next day it happened again. Leaders just began to show up on their lunch breaks and after school. The offices that were once dead and boring, used for discussing budgets, problematic youth, and spreadsheets, were now being used to fill the halls of heaven with praise. When I first started this journey, I had no clue that this would go beyond me, but on the Wednesday night right before service, the group had built up to 100 students and leaders crying out to God in our offices.

Something shifted that week, and it impacted me and our youth ministry forever. There was a new life, a new joy, a new fire that none of us had ever felt before. Our youth ministry began to explode, without flyers or another cool event. Students just began to invite their friends. Within a week's time, we were turning people away because we didn't have room in the building. We started a second service, and that filled up as well. Then God put on my heart to ask our senior pastor if we could move to the main sanctuary, which held 2,500. It was the largest seated auditorium in all of Modesto, California, and God said, "I want to fill it." I asked my senior pastor, and to my surprise there was a resounding yes. Then God put on my heart to prepare for 40 days for what He wanted to do. In response, we opened our first-ever youth prayer room in an abandoned classroom on campus, which we called "The

Round Room." For 40 days and 40 nights, leaders signed up to take hours on end to cry out for a generation to know Jesus. I'll never forget the walls of that prayer room. There wasn't an inch left without a name of an uncle or aunt, brother or sister, mom or dad. Both prayer requests and praise reports to God were etched into those walls. After 40 days and 40 nights, something started inside of us that was much bigger than any of us could imagine.

When we moved into the main sanctuary, we renamed our youth ministry "The Stadium." The name had two meanings for us. First, it was in honor of the early Church believers, who were brought into stadiums in Rome to die for their faith. We would be brought into this stadium to die to ourselves and live for Christ. Secondly, we had a vision of stadiums being full of people worshipping God, and this was the beginning. The first night we opened The Stadium, around 700 students came; 300 of them were new. Many gave their lives to Jesus for the first time that night. From then on, the supernatural continued to take place weekly. We saw radical salvations and miracles. Students turned in tons of stuff after the services: gang rags, drugs, knives, you name it. One night we brought out a giant trash can and wrote "The Devil's Trash Can" on it. Every week, teenagers and young adults threw things in there that they no longer needed in their new life with Jesus. This was it. This was what we had believed for. This was what we saw in our wildest dreams. The funny thing was that this was available to us the whole time. All we had to do was open the door. It felt as if we had unlocked something that could not be shut. We had found an important key in the Kingdom— prayer. God says, "I will give you the keys of the kingdom of heaven; whatever you bind on earth will be bound in heaven, and whatever you loose on earth will be loosed in heaven" (Matt. 16:18). If prayer changes things, then prayerlessness keeps things the way they are. Many are still waiting on God, but I tell you today God is waiting on you. He has given you the keys; it's time we start using them.

IN GOD I TRUST; I AM NOT AFRAID.
WHAT CAN A MERE MORTAL DO TO
ME?

PSALM 56:11

THE ALTARED

10

CHAPTER

Truly, truly, I say to you, unless a grain of wheat
falls into the earth and dies, it remains alone; but
if it dies, it bears much fruit *(John 12:24 ESV)*.

Don't be afraid of detours God ordains. It's worth saying again the best way to live the fearless life is to live it dead. We need a return of the living dead, a rave at the grave, a dawn of the dead. Sounds morbid, so let me explain. While planting a church, God has brought us amazing leaders, ones who stick around. The only thing I can see different in them from the rest of the congregation is that they are dead to themselves. Because of our lack of maturity, church has become a "bless me" club. People who come to church ask questions such as, "Will this church work for me?" "Do they have the right programs for my family?" "Does the pastor preach like I want them to preach?" "Do you believe in the things I want to believe in and see the Bible the way I see the Bible?" These are all great questions that demand an answer. These are normal questions to have when looking for a church. However, because these have become our main focus, we have forgotten what it means to be the Church. We simply go to church. The first church did not live for programs or seating arrangements. They became living sacrifices. Their lives were laid on the altar. When you look at it this way, the Upper Room looks more like an altar with fire than just a church service. From that moment on, they were like the walking dead, continually bringing their lives back to the altar. They had one heart and mind and shared everything they owned. There were no needy people among them (Acts 4:32–35). Wow, what a church. What a movement! Jesus said that this kind of death brings much fruit, fruit that remains. We need to take to heart what John the Baptist said, "He must become greater; I must become less" (John 3:30).

Here in America, we have to understand that Jesus didn't die to make us comfortable; He died to set us free. Many churches are missing the altar. The problem with no altars is that few are altered. Paul did not preach with wise or persuasive words, but with a demonstration of the Spirit's power. How are we demonstrating the Spirit's power unless we get out of the way? As a kid, I don't remember my pastor's sermons, but I do remember the moments when God touched my life at an altar. If we use wise and persuasive words alone, we become more like salesmen than shepherds. What are we selling? What Jesus offers is not for sale. It's not up for auction to the highest bidder. It's a free gift to all who believe.

> JESUS DIDN'T DIE TO MAKE US COMFORTABLE; HE DIED TO SET US FREE.

At times, my focus has been off trying to keep up with the latest church craze. The best way to have a bad Monday is to look at Instagram on Sunday night. You see the highlight reels of every church, but you never see the struggles. In contrast, you see your struggles every day, but you easily forget the highlights. It can make you feel alone and like a failure. However, God is in the struggles and the victories. The greatest victory is to remain obedient to the call. In all of this, I've had to remind myself that while Jesus was alive, He spent the majority of His life with 12 men. Out of the 12, only one was still there at the cross. Success can't be found in numbers alone, in how many new campuses you have, or how fast it grows. It's only found in obedience.

Jesus would say the most radical things to His disciples. Picture the disciples in the moment when Jesus had a massive crowd before Him. Things were finally working out the way the disciples wanted them to. Then, Jesus looked at the crowd and said, "Unless you eat the flesh of the Son of Man and drink his blood, you have no life in you" (John 6:53). After that, He dropped the mic and walked off. He didn't explain it with, "This is what I really meant..." He just walked off. I can picture that Peter probably looked at the other disciples after that moment, confused. I picture the disciples jumping up as people started leaving by the thousands, trying to get them to stay. Jesus looked at the disciples and said, "You do not want to leave too, do you?" (John 6:67).

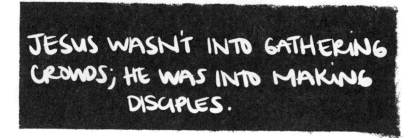

JESUS WASN'T INTO GATHERING CROWDS; HE WAS INTO MAKING DISCIPLES.

Jesus wasn't into gathering crowds; He was into making disciples. Visiting many churches, I have noticed that there are very few places that still have altar moments when people have an opportunity to respond to the message. We often do this because we believe people want safe, clean, comfortable encounters with Jesus. If we want a 21st-century Jesus who makes us comfortable, we may not want who Jesus really is.

There is one thing that my Jesus has never made me, and that's comfortable. He's given me grace, He's given me comfort, He's given me hope as an anchor in many storms, and He's given me peace in chaos. But He is not trying to make me comfortable.

In the Bible, the altar was a place of death. New Testament death equals repentance, brokenness, sacrifice, and humility. As broken clouds bring rain, it's a broken seed that brings forth a crop. As the Church, we are always believing for revival in our cities. I don't believe revival is simply God moving, because, to revive something means to "restore to life or consciousness." God is not dead; He's always alive. God is not boring, we are. God is not being revived, we're being revived, so revival is not God moving. Number one, how can God move if He is omnipresent? How could He move from one place to another? That would be as if we were saying that God is not somewhere and we're waiting for Him to show up there. The Bible says, "The earth is the Lord's, and the fulness thereof" (Ps. 24:1 KJV). God is everywhere all the time. The issue is not about God moving; the issue is about us moving from unbelief to belief, from flesh to spirit. It is about us being revived, not Him. The focus changes from us trying to wake God up, to God waking us up. God's not asleep, we are. Really what's happened is that we've removed the blanket of flesh from our eyes and from our spirit, and for the first time we see the God who was always there. Why do we need to see God? Because seeing is believing. We know that fire doesn't fall on empty altars. If we want the fire of God, we might just have to be the fuel on His altar. John Wesley was once asked how such great crowds showed up during the Great Awakening. He said, "I set myself on fire and people come to watch me burn."

THE
MASTER OF
BROKEN
PIECES

CHAPTER **11**

Life is like a 1,000-piece puzzle, opened, and slowly dumped out, piece by piece. The perfect picture, printed on the box for all to see, is no longer in view as the contents of the box are spread out. Maybe it's been discarded as trash, thrown away, and the memory of it is slowly fading. The hopeless feeling of being left with broken pieces is inescapable, seemingly without the power to put the pieces back together. All the pieces are searching for meaning to the mess, but trying to find identity in the brokenness is impossible.

In our brokenness we attempt the impossible feat of putting ourselves back together. Our previously big dreams and used-to-be secure identities slowly fade, and we are left with the fragments. Did you know that we can praise God for the fragments, though? If it weren't for the fragments, we may stop searching. It is the brokenness that points you to a greater purpose and won't let you stop searching. A part of you was cut here, and another part was cut there. Maybe your innocence was stolen from you here or you were rejected. Maybe someone touched you in places they shouldn't have. Maybe you didn't receive the affection you needed. Now, because of hands that wronged you, you either end up in everyone's hands or run from hands altogether, isolating yourself from people. Maybe it was the hurt they caused when they called you "loser." If it was just another person on the street or even an acquaintance, you could have handled it, but it was your dad and it stuck. You can see nothing but "loser" now when you look in the mirror. No matter what you achieve, it's never enough because the wound goes deep into your identity; you've been marked.

Maybe it's not what they said, but what they didn't say. They never once said, "Good job" or "I'm proud of you." The words "I love you" always had expectations attached to them, and you never quite performed well enough to please them. Feeling like a mess, you look for something that looks nothing like you to heal your brokenness. You're broken and cut, and so you find another box with a beautiful picture on the front. *Adding them will give me purpose and value again,* you think. After some time, you find out that they, too, are just broken pieces on the inside. Many people think that adding a relationship to the mix will solve their problems. They think having a significant other will complete them or make them whole, but they eventually find out that is not true. When two broken people come together, they just end up with more broken pieces. Now they're carrying the other person's brokenness in addition to their own. One person is always trying to put the other person back together. This can feel overwhelming. Many times, this is what happens within marriage. A broken man and a broken woman come together thinking the magic of marriage will solve all their problems, only to discover that it created more. Then, they add some kids thinking that will heal their marriage and make things better, only to find that they've passed on their brokenness to their children. With a whole house of broken pieces, life feels like a mess. Maybe you're one of those kids who was born into this kind of environment. Maybe your world feels so hopelessly broken that you don't even know where to start. In no way am I saying marriage or family is the problem. I, myself am married and have kids. Those just aren't the solution to brokenness.

Here's one thing we all know about puzzles: they cannot put themselves together. It takes the expertise of an outside hand and an artistic eye to masterfully place the pieces together, fulfilling the puzzle's original purpose: to reflect the beautiful picture on the front of the box. It takes someone who can see the big picture and the individual pieces at the same time. There is not anyone who can see both like Jesus can. The beautiful thing about Jesus is that He is that outside hand, with an eye to see the beginning, middle, and end at the same time. He alone has the power to put you back together.

I love that when you look at a puzzle that has been put back together, the picture is not what awes you. Most of the time the picture is not that significant. Maybe it's a picture of a hot air balloon over a sunset, a black stallion in its natural habitat, or an old house on the edge of a river. Those are all beautiful things, but the real beauty is found in the number of pieces that were placed back together and in the artist and his skill level to complete such a thing. The more broken pieces there were, the more in awe we are of the master of the piece. This same thing happens in our lives. It's not the life and destiny we live out; it's that we shouldn't be able to do it. We were broken beyond repair with no hope; we were lost. Then Jesus stepped in and was the Master of the piece, making us His masterpiece. Ephesians 2:10 (NLT) says it beautifully:

> For we are God's masterpiece. He has created us anew in Christ Jesus, so we can do the good things he planned for us long ago.

An artist's masterpiece is a piece of work that is considered the greatest work of the artist's career. It's a work of outstanding creativity and skill that shows the artist's great workmanship. The creator of the piece, not the creation itself, determines when the piece is done and how it looks in the end. How funny is it when the creation tells the Creator He messed up when creating it. When we demean a painting, we don't just put down the painting; we put down the artist. You didn't paint yourself, God did, and He didn't make any mistakes. You are His masterpiece. It's time to believe what He said about you and live out His glorious plans for your life.

Let's give glory to the Master of the piece by entrusting the broken pieces of our lives back into His hands. As long as we hold on to the pieces and try to put them together ourselves, we delay what God alone has the power to do. If you want to save your life, if you want your life restored to the picture God intended, you will find it when you hand all the hurt and all the wounds—your pieces—back to Him. He alone is able to take all our pieces and put them together in a way that displays His greatness to everyone around you.

> For whoever wants to save their life will lose it, but whoever loses their life for me will find it (Matthew 16:25).

GOD SEES YOU

God wants to give us new eyes. For so long, I prayed for God to show up in my life. I would wait hours for Him to show up in prayer meetings and worship services, but one day God rocked me in my hotel room while I was waiting to speak to a youth camp. I was doing what I always did, begging for God to be there that night in the service. This was my usual. One hour before any service, I would cry out, not for a generation, but for the presence of God to invade the service. Well, that day, the voice of God shot through the room. I was in the presence of God immediately. He said, "Jeremy, why are you begging Me to show up tonight? I'm here. I love you. It hurts My heart when you beg. Don't you know I'm a good Dad?" I answered, "Yes, Father, I know You're an incredible Dad." "Then why do you keep treating Me like I'm a distant Father, unwilling to be with you?"

Then, the Holy Spirit took me back to six months prior. It was one of the greatest moments of my life. I became a father for the first time, to Lyric Noel Love Johnson, a 6-pound 5-ounce beautiful baby girl. I never knew I could love a person as much as I loved this little child. The unique thing was that Lyric had done nothing to earn my love. In fact, my love was much more powerful than her performance. It went beyond performance; it was deep in my soul. I didn't love Lyric because she was beautiful, although to me she was the most beautiful baby in the whole nursery. I loved her because she was mine. I was somewhat irritated that God brought Lyric to my mind, because instantly my thoughts began to wander from the service. I was thinking about those beautiful little eyes and the way she looked at me as her dad. Then I heard the voice of God say, "Will Lyric ever have to beg you to be at anything?" Instantly, I responded back to God, "No way! In fact, I can't wait until she needs me. Just the slightest cry and I'm in. I dream of the day she starts soccer or ballet, not so she can be the best, but so I can show her that I'm the best dad. That no matter what she does or how she performs, I'm both her protector and biggest fan."

The very thought of her brought a "new dad smile" to my face. Then the Lord spoke, "Then why do you beg Me to be here tonight? I'm a dad. I'm on the front row, on the edge of My seat cheering you on, not because you're perfect, but because you're mine." In that moment I thought of all the times I felt alone in the journey. "God, where were you then?" He shot back, "I was there, just your eyes could not see Me. All they saw was what was in the natural, but I am supernatural. How can I move in or out of any place if I'm omnipresent? If I moved, it would mean I would have to leave one place to invade another that I wasn't in, but I am everywhere all the time. Son, I don't move, I manifest, and I manifest where I'm honored."

It's the enemy's ultimate deception when he gets you to unknowingly dishonor God's fatherhood. The enemy is happy when you call God "Father" but see Him through the lens of your earthly father's humanity and failures. In order for us to truly see God as a father, we have to get new eyes.

> *In the last days, God says, I will pour out my Spirit on all people. Your sons and daughters will prophesy, your young men will see visions, your old men will dream dreams. Even on my servants, both men and women, I will pour out my Spirit in those days, and they will prophesy* [Acts 2:17-18].

This Scripture is quoting Joel 2:28, and the original Hebrew word for "to see" is *rā'â*, which has many significant meanings when looking at this verse. It means, "to look at each other, to face, meet, enjoy, have experience."

This word is also used in Genesis 1:4, when "God saw that the light was good." In this verse, we understand that God was experiencing the light He saw. It wasn't just in His imagination; it was real. It was tangible. If we were there with God, we would be experiencing it with our senses. So when the Scripture says young men will see visions, it doesn't mean that we will just see them from far off and hope to one day live in them. Instead, in the last days, young men will encounter the reality of their visions. Their visions will be something they touch. In other words, young men will shake hands with what they see and be found in it. So the question is not if you see a vision, but what vision you see, and what you see is what you'll find, whether good or bad. Your perception will become your reality. Whatever you're looking at, even if it's from far off, will eventually become something you touch if you continue to look in that direction. Henry Ford, the founder of Ford Motor Company, and someone who revolutionized the auto industry said it this way: "Whether you think you can, or you think you can't, you're right."

In Numbers 13, Moses sends out spies to check out what the Promised Land was like. Caleb was one of those spies. He and the rest of the spies visited the same land. They saw the same things. They lived in the same dream, but they had different perspectives of themselves. What they saw was more powerful than what they were in; ultimately, what you see is what you'll be found in. All the enemy has to do is change the lens through which you see the goodness of God, and you will miss what God has for you. You'll end up rejecting the very thing that God is giving you just like the spies did.

Recently, Fearless BND wrote a song, and these lyrics ring true for all of us: "Finally I can see what You saw. You believed in me. The love inside, the eyes set on fire staring back at me."

God is the painter, and we are the painting. Take a look at everything God ever made. Look at the sun. It's 93 million miles away, one giant ball of gas. It's close enough to warm our days, far enough to cool our nights, and it's the perfect distance away so that we don't disintegrate under its heat. It's but one of God's creations, yet we still can't duplicate it. Scientists try to create even a portion of the energy it disperses, and they fail. Yet God spoke and it came to pass. No one had ever seen the sun or created one, but God in the recesses of His mind imagined this as the center of our solar system, and by simply speaking "Let there be light," it became. God's creation is incredible, from the galactic magnitude of the solar systems to the delicate finiteness of the budding of a flower, to how bees carry pollen from one flower to the next, to the human body. Your eyes reading this page right now are connected to 120 million rods and cones, sending signals into your brain, constructing thoughts, ideas, words, and sentences. Your heart is beating, your breath is filling your lungs. This God is a creative, ingenious, original all by Himself kind of God, yet when the Master Creator is given the opportunity to pick from all of His creations which one He would like to be remembered for, He chose you and me. He deemed us as the pinnacle of His creation, His masterpiece.

One of my favorite painters is Vik Muniz. His creativity does not allow him to be average. While others were using their paint and paintbrushes to show off their limited skills, he was using peanut butter, jelly, and a knife to create art. One of his first paintings was the Mona Lisa using half peanut butter and half jelly. He is a creative. One of his later pieces was a throwback to a childhood piece. He went to one of the largest garbage dumps in the world, took trash and created aerial-viewed-only paintings of people who are labeled "garbage pickers." They would show up to the garbage dump and look for treasure amongst the trash. This style of art was a throwback to his days on his mom's kitchen floor where he would pull the trash out of the trash can and align it in perfect proximity to a light that he set up. The light would cast against the trash, and it would cast a shadow from the trash, forming a picture. It was only with his masterful eyes that he could see the masterpiece in the broken pieces. Creatives enjoy doing more with less. You could say the same for God. He finds great joy in taking what others could not use and doing something extraordinary with it.

> HE FINDS GREAT JOY IN TAKING WHAT OTHERS COULD NOT USE AND DOING SOMETHING EXTRAORDINARY WITH IT.

See, I don't know about you, but God saw me when no one else did. It was Him and Him alone who chose me when the world ran out on me, when they were done with me. When they thought all my potential was used up, they threw me away, and it was His hand that was bold enough and brave enough to reach into my mess and create a message in me. When God looks at what Jesus did with our lives, as the painter of the picture He says, "That is My greatest masterpiece," and not only are you a masterpiece, but you were made in the image of His Son. When He sees you, He doesn't see trash anymore; He sees a new picture of Jesus.

ONLY FEAR THE LORD, AND SERVE
HIM FAITHFULLY WITH ALL YOUR
HEART; FOR CONSIDER WHAT GREAT
THINGS HE HAS DONE FOR YOU.

1 SAMUEL 12:24

IDENTITY
CHECK

CHECK

12

As a person whose love language is words of affirmation, I tend to gravitate toward people who encourage me. Words really impact me, so the enemy uses negative words and thoughts to get me to believe lies about myself, and more often than not, he succeeds. Since I tend to lean toward the negative side of things, the Word of God and the words of others give life to me during these battles. Encouraging words are like fuel in my tank. I've found that having people in your life who will celebrate you and not just tolerate you can be the driving force you need to advance in what God is calling you to. One of those people in my life is Pat Schatzline; God has used him in some of the craziest moments in my life to help me get up one more time. Whenever he came to speak at our church, I would volunteer to be his driver to take him from meeting to meeting. There would always be a moment when the Holy Spirit would use him to help remind me not to give up. Whenever I left his presence, I felt like I could conquer hell with just a water pistol. You need those people in your life.

In one of our conversations, I was in a vulnerable place. I was feeling beat up by some of the other staff members at our church. I felt unheard and wrongly judged with some situations that happened with the youth. Most of the youth coming to our church were in the habit of leaving places dirty. We would have a great night, but the next day instead of talking about the hundreds of salvations that took place, the only thing the staff would talk about was how the bathrooms were a mess. When I look back at some of the things that ran through my head back then, I think, *Wow, how foolish was I that I couldn't see beyond my ministry?* However, when you are growing in your calling, you learn and mature as you go.

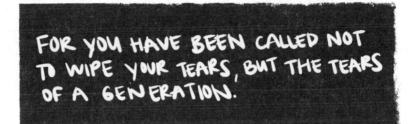

FOR YOU HAVE BEEN CALLED NOT TO WIPE YOUR TEARS, BUT THE TEARS OF A GENERATION.

As I poured out my heart to Pat, I saw the love in his eyes and knew he was going to give me something that would put me back on track. Pat said, "Pull over the car." When we got out of the car and were standing on the side of the road, Pat got something out of his bag. I thought, *What could this be? I've never gotten a physical gift of encouragement before.* Pat walked up to the front of the car where I was standing; he was holding a small red handkerchief in his hand. He put it in my hands and said, "Now close your eyes." Then he began to minister to me. He said, "Wipe up your tears. Today's the last day you are allowed to cry over yourself. You don't have time. You have not been called and chosen by God to cry over what you didn't get, to what people didn't see in you. Jeremy, when they misjudge you or misunderstand you, don't let that rob you. For you have been called not to wipe your tears, but the tears of a generation. Every time you waste a moment on your tears, you cannot see their tears. Jeremy, make it your duty that every time the devil tries to get you to cry over yourself, you look up and say, 'I will not let him detour me from the high call of wiping up the tears of a generation.'" That day I made a choice, not that I would never cry again, but that my tears would move in a different direction. I would cry for the abandoned, the broken, and the hurting. When I wasn't crying for or crying out over them, I would use this rag to wipe up their tears. It was as if a red flag was waving at me that day reminding me of why I began this journey in the first place, of why God called me.

Today, what are your eyes focused on? Are they on what you didn't get, that people misjudged you, or how they rejected you? I have brought this lesson with me into every battle within my head. I have taken that rag into many arenas, camps, and conferences and wiped the tears of those who needed someone who had moved beyond his own tears. How can I get my eyes off of me, you ask? This question is the main reason why we remain stuck, isn't it? Why we can't see past the rejection and the judgments into the real hurt of the person on the other end of the pain. Most reject you not because of you but because of their own insecurities.

Have you ever gone into an Apple store? When you walk in, you can feel the excitement of the employees who are ready to help. When one of our leaders got a job there, I asked him, "How in the world do they have such great customer service?" The workers always seem to be in a good mood, and I wanted to know the secret. I know from years of training leaders that this is no easy task. His response was, "It was simple. They showed us an animated cartoon called The Present." I was so intrigued by this that I looked up the cartoon, and I was blown away by what I saw. It was so simple, yet so profound. It was a video that caused all of the Apple employees to think about others instead of themselves. The mini-film starts with a young boy playing a video game. You can hear shooting in the game; by the look on the boy's face, you can see that it's an intense game. His mom enters through the front door with a small box; she drops the box next to the boy on the couch and then walks into the kitchen. The boy seems to be so focused on his game that he doesn't notice the gift. His mom peeks her head around the corner and says, "Why don't you stop playing and open the present I got for you?" After pausing his game, he opens the box, and all of a sudden, a puppy's head pops out. The boy's eyes light up, "Woah! Cool!" But as he pulls the puppy out of the box, he discovers that the puppy has only three legs. One leg is just a nub. The boy's face goes from excitement to disgust. He throws the puppy and the box to the floor, and he goes right back to playing his game. The puppy sees a red ball that had fallen out of the box; he gets the ball and returns to the boy's side. The boy kicks the ball away from him, and the puppy chases it again. A second time, the puppy brings the ball back to the boy. The boy stands to his feet and grabs the crutches that were on the couch, and as the boy stands, you see that the boy is also missing a leg. The boy and the dog hobble to the door and go outside to play.[1]

A wave of emotions hit me when watching this short film. What a simple thought; there is always more to the story. People don't reject you because of you; there is something hidden that causes nice people to be angry. You must be like that puppy, not focused on the rejection, but persisting in loving the other person. You never know what kind of day, month, year, or life they have had that has rendered them helpless against negative thinking. It's not my job to receive their rejection as mine. It's my job to love them through it. There is always more to the story, there is always hope, and love will always win against hate. Perfect love casts out all fear, and that perfect love is the unconditional love that only Jesus can help us walk in.

Words are like arrows, piercing our souls. It's as if they are shot by expert marksmen, with precise aim, into the depths of our souls. I'm not trying to sound dramatic; however, it usually is. It's not often that some far-off enemy or unseen force attacks us. These attacks usually come through an up-close, face-to-face encounter. Someone wounded you while they looked you in the eyes. It's not likely that they were an enemy, but a friend, someone who told you they loved you, that they would always be there. Maybe for you, it was a parent, a leader, or even a sibling. Maybe it was a son or a daughter that caused the greatest pain. Once the arrow went in, the pain sent you into such shock that you were not able to fully comprehend what happened. When the pain becomes overwhelming, most of us find ourselves retreating to a place of safety. I'm not sure what safety walls you have built, but some of mine have been anger, avoidance, and isolation.

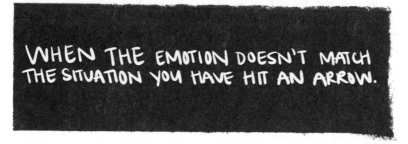

WHEN THE EMOTION DOESN'T MATCH THE SITUATION YOU HAVE HIT AN ARROW.

For years, I ran for the hills and forgot to do one thing: remove the arrow. The pain of the arrow hurt so bad in the first place that many times I left the arrow inside of me, thinking, *One day when I feel like it, I will remove it.* This is when the enemy wins, because now his true poison can start working. The wound eventually heals, but we are left with this arrow of bitterness, fear, shame, and insecurity. The memory brings pain long after the person is gone. Even though the incident happened long ago and we've convinced ourselves that we've moved on, we moved on without removing the arrow. We keep the pain attached to the memory.

Every time someone gets close to us, the arrow is bumped or nudged, and the pain begins all over again. You may have had your arrow bumped or bump someone else's arrow. I've found myself saying, "I don't know what I said to make them react like this." It's not what you said; it's what they haven't forgiven. When the emotion doesn't match the situation you have hit an arrow. We can't forget that every person has a backstory. The person that stands in front of us now is a makeup of every heartache, every letdown, and every victory. I'll never forget William George III. It was my junior year at Bible college when I met William. He caught my attention. Every day in the cafeteria when others would find a crowd to sit with, William would look for an empty table to eat alone. His demeanor was cold and scared; he kept his head down when walking from class to class. He had a shaved head, thick glasses, and wore a kilt every day. William was so interesting to me that I couldn't help but to find out what this guy was all about.

Every day I would make it my goal to try to sit or walk with William. Every attempt ended in failure. Every time I tried to have a conversation or sit down with him, he would ignore me or walk away. I wasn't going to give up easy, I made it my special duty to try to find a way into William George's life. One afternoon he was walking up to our dorm rooms, and

I was playing pool. William saw me and picked up the pace, acting as if he didn't see me. I yelled out, "William, play me one round." If you win, I'll leave you alone and never try to talk to you again. But if I win, you have to let me take you to lunch and actually have a conversation with me." William uttered the first words he had ever said to me, "You're on."

What I didn't know is that William figured he would beat me since he had played on the pool team all throughout high school. I have no clue why I challenged him to a pool contest since I was horrible at pool. It was the first thing that popped into my mind, but hey, if God could make it rain fire from heaven with Elijah, then He could help me beat William George III. It made me nervous when William came back down with a personalized cue stick to start the game. It must have been the Holy Spirit playing with me, though, because everyone of William's shots missed and all of mine made it. Elijah had fire on a mountain, but I had fire on the table. I cleaned house that day. As the last ball went in, I saw the look of fear on William's face when he realized he would have to hold up to his end of the bargain.

The very next day I took William out to a proper college student lunch at Subway. For the first time, with tears in his eyes, William opened up to me. I was blown away with his story. He lost his parents at a young age, and when he was a junior in high school, he lost his girlfriend in a gang-related, drive-by shooting. Those two painful experiences caused William to make a vow with fear that he would never let anyone in again, he'd never get close to anyone. He believed that if he kept people at a distance, it wouldn't hurt when they weren't there. The moment William opened up his heart to me, I understood more why he was the way he was. His fear of me had nothing to do with me and everything to do with what happened. From that moment, William and I began what would turn out to be a great friendship. However, it took lots of patience. Fear does not come just to take away your future; it comes to take away your present by keeping you looking at the past. Fear keeps your eyes on the pain trying to avoid ever experiencing pain again. Later in college, I started a ministry with other college students sharing their testimony, and I saw William get to share his story with so many others. He took his eyes off pain and put them on healing so he could embrace a fearless life. Sometimes it's not easy to fight the war on fear, but the fearless life is always worth it.

Unknowingly, many live miserable lives thinking everyone is out to hurt them, and they can't figure out why the pain they thought they had victory over keeps coming back in new situations. Forgiveness isn't saying they didn't hurt you; it's saying, "I don't want to live with your hurt anymore." It's dismissing the lie that you have allowed to become your truth. Many times I have bought into the lies from my past hook, line, and sinker.

A lot of arrows are cleverly shot before you reach five years of age. According to psychologists, these are the formative years. At this young age, we don't have the cognitive sense to understand how broken it truly is until it hurts us, of course. So, we make choices based on our perception of the world and the people we meet in it; these choices stick with us for the rest of our lives. Whether they are true or not, what we believe in those formative years creates the foundation for our overall belief system. We believe what we believe because of our experience. What we miss is the fact that the reasoning skills of a child have been the basis of how we formed our worldview. The enemy is sly to introduce things into the lives of those who will set others free at a young age. He locks them up in hopes that as long as they never get free, those around them will also stay bound.

Fear traps you, and fear can make you immature in areas of your life. That immaturity holds you back and won't allow you to move forward. To those around you, the fear can look like you are rebelling against God's call, but it is actually fear perpetuated by a lie you believe. Although it looks like disobedience, it is simply immaturity. A great friend once told me, "Disobedience and immaturity look the same, but we as leaders must handle them differently." When we deal with disobedience, we must deal strongly with it. We know that the one qualification of the first church was obedience. It was their great obedience that allowed them to walk in great power. Before God opened the windows of heaven and poured Himself out on the first church, they were tested in the area of obedience. We see this after Jesus died and rose again. He sat on a hill, revealing Himself to over 500 followers after fulfilling what He said He would do. Jesus told them that before they could receive power, they must do one thing. They must go back to Jerusalem and wait until they were clothed with power. He could've given them the power right then and there, but He decided that there was an initial thing they must do.

The next thing we see is the disciples in the Upper Room, where there are 120 people. However, on the hillside where Jesus challenged them, there were 500. That means 380 people were disobedient to a direct order from the risen Jesus, who they had just seen with their own eyes. God wants to release His power on this earth, but He knows power not under authority is bad news. Power without guidance is no different than a race car without a steering wheel. Power without direction is dangerous, and so is a person who doesn't make room for guidance in their life. Even Jesus Himself said over and over again, "Not my will, but yours be done" (Luke 22:42).

When Jesus taught His disciples to pray, He told them to say, "Your kingdom come, your will be done, on earth as it is in heaven" (Matt. 6:10). When Jesus was struggling in the Garden of Gethsemane with His will over the Father's, the fight was on, and Jesus won by losing. He chose to honor His Father's will above His own. During Jesus's life on earth, Jesus said it was His food to do the will of He who sent Him, and that it was His great joy to finish His work (John 4:34). We know that Romans 5:19 says, "For just as through the disobedience of the one man the many were made sinners, so also through the obedience of the one man the many will be made righteous." In 1 Samuel 15:23 (NKJV), we see that "rebellion is as the sin of witchcraft, and stubbornness is as iniquity and idolatry. Because you have rejected the word of the Lord, He also has rejected you." The verse right before this tells us that the Lord is not pleased with burnt offerings or sacrifices, but instead by obedience. Obedience is better than sacrifice.

Power without obedience is like a large ship without a rudder. It's power with no guidance. Also, notice that the faster you go, the more careful you have to be with your guidance systems. Have you ever seen one of those speed boat races? In a matter of a few seconds, the boat, having a 1,000 horsepower engine, speeds up to 200 mph, and with the slightest wobble of the jet strap on this tiny boat, it flips through the air, ripping apart. Most of us have kept the engine removed from the guidance system, and this is why many have shipwrecked their faith. As the great theologian, Spider-Man, once said, "With great power comes great responsibility." Someone once told me that responsibility can be defined as "our response to His ability." In other words, the more we respond by obeying the Word of God, the more we walk in His ability, not our own.

Just a reminder, though, that immaturity and disobedience look the same, but they should be handled differently. When most people look at the Church of today and our generation, most see a bunch of stubborn-hearted, rebellious people. Do you know what God sees, though? God sees a bunch of sons and daughters that have been wounded. The enemy would hate for us to walk in the high call that's on our lives. He would love for us to stay confined as adults, with parts of our hearts still stuck at four or five years old. We must remove these chains, get healing for our triggers, and grow out of our immaturities swiftly so we can move on to accomplish the call God has for us.

I didn't have the horrible childhood that so many young people have today. A lot of them have had such a tough go. They were abused or molested at the hands of someone they trusted. I can't even imagine the pain that would bring. My story was a lot simpler. I allowed the lies the enemy said about me to become my truth. It doesn't have to be a major thing that sets us on the wrong path; many times, it's simple. My parents had the opportunity to hold me back or send me to school early because of my age; they chose to send me to kindergarten early. As a result, I was the smallest kid in my class. The other kids loved to point out that I was smaller than them. We kids didn't understand that I was smaller only because I was younger. The teacher who was trying to protect me urged my parents to hold me back a year to catch up. She could see that moving forward would keep me behind in more areas than my size. My mom and dad, being the loving parents they are, were instantly offended at the teacher for even suggesting such a thing. "No, my son won't be held back because of some teacher who doesn't know how to teach," they said. My mom told me as a young boy, "Son, don't worry about what the teacher says; we're not going to hold you back. You're just different, and that's okay." Somehow when hearing those words, I bought into the lie that whenever I felt like I was behind, as long as I could run into the shelter of being different, I would find my identity. The only bad thing about this is that no matter how different I became, it was never enough to fulfill the true longing for identity that I had. It could only be found in Christ. Only recently, have I learned that I still have those triggers in my life. Whenever I feel behind "the rest of the class," I try to find comfort in being different, to feel better about not fitting into the crowd around me. I'm not saying that it's a bad thing to be different or to stand out, but God didn't create you to fit in, so why start now? We are not mass produced to get the greatest return value. Our Father has handcrafted us; each one of us is different, and it will take us a lifetime to fully discover who He made us to be. However, I learned that first we need to remove the lies so we can find the truth.

The truth God recently revealed to me is that identity in the Kingdom is not something that is formed but discovered. A friend of mine who has a prophetic gift on his life had a dream about me. In the dream, he saw me standing in a field, feverishly searching the area around my feet. He said it was like I was consumed with finding the thing that was missing, so consumed that nothing else mattered. He knew that whatever it was must've been of great value. Then, out of nowhere in the dream, I stopped and focused on a specific area of the field. There was an excitement as I lifted a jewel off of the ground. I studied the jewel for a few minutes, then put it in my pocket. In the next picture he saw, I was dressed in beautiful, shiny armor. At first, when my friend told me this dream, I had no clue what it meant. What, if anything, was God trying to say to me through this strange dream? What was I looking for? Was I searching for something? If I was, I didn't realize it. What was so important that it would consume my life? Once I found it, would it really give me the courage to stand dressed in the armor God designed for me? This jewel was my identity. Finally, at 38 years old, I realize that a jewel is the best symbol of my identity.

Identity is like a jewel that is dug up from the ground; when the layers of grime and filth are removed, it can be revealed in its full beauty and value. Our true identity isn't something that can be added to or subtracted from. It cannot grow or be developed; it can only be discovered. The jewel is multifaceted. When light shines on it, more of what was already there is revealed. Every day is an adventure filled with new things to discover. Life is an ongoing classroom where you can discover the "you" God designed. As life turns the hands of time, and as I walk through situations, I find more facets of what He created—things that have always been there but are just now being discovered.

In the proper light, a jewel's beauty is revealed to the entire room. Not only does the enemy want to keep us from discovering our true identities, but he would love to keep it in the dark. If you ever discovered your true identity, his lies would lose their power instantly. So, to keep the beauty in us a secret, he causes us to hide like Adam did in the garden, finding anything we can to clothe our nakedness. Every day, I am discovering the beauty He made in me before this world conformed me to a pattern. We have been programmed to think that identity is inseparable from behavior, but God doesn't look at it that way. He determines identity not from behavior, but from birth and through relationship. Second Corinthians 5:17 says, "Therefore, if anyone is in Christ, he is a new creation; old things have passed away; behold, all things have become new" (NKJV). The root word of *creation* in this Scripture is the Greek word *ktizō*, meaning "to create." This word does not mean to give something a facelift or to improve something that already exists; it implies creating something for the first time. God didn't merely change us when we were saved; He created a whole new person. Ephesians 2:1 tells us that we were dead in trespasses and sins, both our own and of others. In other words, we crossed the line, and sin caused us death. It was your spirit that was dead. You are a spirit that lives in a body and has a soul. Inside your soul is your mind, will, and emotions. It's hard to lead your soul with a dead captain. This is why God brings life to your dead spirit. It's the Spirit of Christ that now lives in you.

The world struggles to find meaning and purpose for their lives, searching for it with their bodies and in their souls. They miss the fact that identity cannot be found in your body; your body only gives you world-consciousness—the things around you, the life you lead, the house you live in, the car you drive, the people you date, the zeros in your paycheck, the ability to feel hot and cold. You will not find meaning in your soul alone, either. It's not found in how you think, how you feel, or what you choose. Your true identity can only be found in your spirit. We search to find meaning, but meaning can only be found when your spirit is made alive in Christ, when you are raised from death to life and born again. In that new birth, your true identity is revealed as a child of the Most High God. Colossians 3:4 states, "And when Christ, who is your life, is revealed to the whole world, you will share in all his glory" (NLT). Your identity is now found in Christ alone. Your identity is not found in your feelings, which is why you sometimes will not feel like you are who God says you are. You have to decide if you are going to trust your feelings or if you are going to trust His Word. Why is identity so important? It is because no person can continuously behave in a way that is inconsistent with the way he perceives himself. Knowing who God is and knowing who we are in Him are the two most important truths we will ever possess. If we believe we are ugly, dumb, and worthless, then it will be impossible to live as if we are beautiful, smart, or valuable.

I'm reminded of a story by an unknown author that goes something like this:

> As my friend was passing some elephants, he suddenly stopped, confused by the fact that these huge creatures were being held by only a small rope tied to their front leg. No chains, no cages. It was

obvious that the elephants could, at any time, break away from the ropes they were tied to but for some reason, they did not. My friend saw a trainer nearby and asked why these beautiful, magnificent animals just stood there and made no attempt to get away.

"Well," he said, "when they are very young and much smaller, we use the same size of rope to tie them and, at that age, it's enough to hold them. As they grow up, they are conditioned to believe they cannot break away. They believe the rope can still hold them, so they never try to break free." My friend was amazed. These animals could at any time break free from their bonds but because they believed they couldn't, they were stuck right where they were.

These gigantic, powerful creatures had limited their present abilities because of the limitations of the past. The elephants became so accustomed to being held back by a rope, that a mere rope itself kept them in check. If they only knew their true identity and how powerful they really were. If only they realized that a rope secured to a pole could no longer hold them back. Then they would know what true freedom is. Sadly, they don't.

Our identity in Christ is one of the most liberating truths we will ever experience. Let me ask you a question: On a scale from 1 to 10, how would you rate your level of acceptance with God? If you don't feel accepted by Him, you will have trouble developing intimacy with Him. It's really hard to warm up to someone if they don't like you or accept you. Have you ever begun to dislike a person you sensed didn't particularly like you? Maybe they didn't do anything, but you just felt it. You and I both know that it goes against every fiber in your bones to develop a relationship with somebody you believe hates you. One of satan's most powerful tools is to get Christians to think that God frowns upon them, when in reality He's smiling.

God already accepts us simply because of what Jesus did, but He is also in the business of transforming us. Romans 12:1–2 says:

> *Therefore, I urge you, brothers and sisters, in view of God's mercy, to offer your bodies as a living sacrifice, holy and pleasing to God—this is your true and proper worship. Do not conform any longer to the pattern of this world, but be transformed by the renewing of your mind. Then you will be able to test and approve what God's will is—his good, pleasing and perfect will.*

Transforming is different from conforming. To conform is to fashion oneself according to another's pattern. This is what life and the world around us do, but God longs to reveal who we are to us, transforming us, not conforming us to the world. We are not to be molded to this world's standards but transformed into who He already said we are. Being transformed into something we were always created to be is quite different than to be conformed or molded after a pattern. The word *molded* makes me instantly think of an assembly line and the process it takes for a material to go from being something useless to something great. This is not how God operates. The way God operates is through transformation. The word *transformed* in Romans 12:2 comes from the Greek word, *metamorphoō*, which means "metamorphose." The picture of this word is not something being formed, but something that was always there being revealed through a process. We can see how God operates by looking at the process of metamorphosis that a caterpillar goes through when it's in the cocoon. During the process of cocooning, the caterpillar becomes a butterfly. What is revealed after the process is something that was always inside the caterpillar, but once revealed, the caterpillar became a new creation. I believe this is what God is saying to us: "I want to reveal to you what I finished in you from the beginning." Your identity is already complete in Jesus and your destiny decided. You simply have to leave the moldings of life, man, and religion behind to receive what God wants to reveal to you. Then you can truly stop giving in to fear. Ecclesiastes 6:10 (NLT) makes it really simple:

> Everything has already been decided. It was known long ago what each person would be. So there's no use arguing with God about your destiny.

We know He is not working on something new. He already finished the end product long ago. All we have to do is go to Genesis and look at when He formed the sun. Most would say the sun was created on day one because that's when God said, "Let there be light." Yes, the light was formed on the first day, but the part most people miss is that the sun was not. Genesis 1:3–5 states:

> And God said, "Let there be light," and there was light. God saw that the light was good, and he separated the light from the darkness. God called the light "day," and the darkness he called "night." And there was evening, and there was morning—the first day.

The sun wasn't even formed on the second or third day; God waited until the fourth day to form the sun. Verses 16–19 go onto say:

> God made two great lights—the greater light to govern the day and the lesser light to govern the night. He also made the stars. God set them in the vault of the sky to give light on the earth, to govern the day and the night, and to separate light from darkness. And God saw that it was good. And there was evening, and there was morning—the fourth day.

Isn't that wild? The sun was simply put there to rule over the light God designed, or as verse 16 says, "to govern the day." God longed for something to manage what He finished. He wanted this manager to point to the author and finisher; this is the same with our destiny and our identity. Both are already complete in Him, and now we are stewards of what God designed. When God designs, He starts with perfection with the finished product, and then reveals it backwards. Isaiah 46:10 says:

> I make known the end from the beginning, from ancient times, what is still to come. I say, "My purpose will stand, and I will do all that I please."

It's like a film producer in a movie sitting next to you telling you what happens at the end. He's not guessing or hoping that his words will happen; he's already completed the movie. It's you who is seeing the movie for the first time. So when He says that, He makes known the end from the beginning, the fact that He makes it known is proof that it's already finished.

To take it further, another Scripture that comes to mind is Revelation 13:8, which says, "The Lamb who was slain from the foundation of the world" (NKJV). From the foundation of the world, from the beginning, Jesus was crucified. Before the problem of sin ever existed, He had the solution.

He doesn't start like man starts, with a little here, a little there, working from imperfection to perfection. When God creates, He does it perfectly the first time. The same is true for our destiny and identity, which God designed. Our only job is to discover what He already finished.

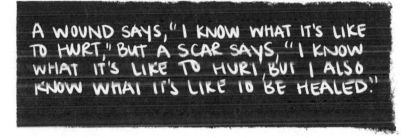

Our job is not to create our path, but to discover it, while removing the arrows or the triggers. Once these arrows are removed, and the pain is separated from the memory, the arrows become weapons in the hands of the warrior at the gates of the enemy. The warrior is you. Spiritually, you are a warrior at the gates of your enemy. The pain will come back, and you may weep like a five-year-old, even if you are 30 years old. The pain often brings you back to that specific time, just for a moment, to bring healing for a lifetime. It's time we let Jesus heal our wounds, turning them into scars. A wound says, "I know what it's like to hurt," but a scar says, "I know what it's like to hurt, but I also know what it's like to be healed." God allowed the wounds so you could preach with your scars. When Jesus showed back up to the disciples, He didn't show them the nails in His hands;

He showed them the scars. It was His scars that they touched, and it was the scars that moved them.

We must catch that God is saying, "Look, I paint differently, I design differently, and I create like no other. So that comes into play when I created you." Look what He says in Isaiah 46:9b, right before He says He knows the end at the beginning:

> I am God, and there is no other; I am God, and there is none like me.

God is trying to tell us that no one compares to Him. He doesn't paint like we paint. Unlike us, He does not work from imperfection to perfection. We work from imperfection to perfection. When we were little, we tried to draw something, and it looked more like scribbles than real designs. Let's just say, our art was always left to interpretation (maybe it still is). When we gave it away as a gift, whoever received the picture said, "Wow, that's incredible! What is it? Is that a dog?" Then we would say, "No, that's you." No matter what we drew, they thought it was beautiful. However, as we grew, the pictures we drew got better. Yet, even when we become experts at something, we don't start with the end product like God does. We start with the raw materials, and with those materials we build what will one day become a masterpiece. Through time, sweat, and tears, we form and shape what we dream of in our minds so others can finally see it. However, this is not how God paints. The first time He does it, it's perfect.

I am complete in Him. How can this be? Sometimes I feel so broken and out of place. God doesn't paint in stick figures and straight lines. He does not draw lines when He sees you. Look at everything God has made. It's not one-dimensional;

it's three dimensional. When God made what He would make, He didn't use lines; He used circles. We keep thinking our destiny is a straight line. We think, "When I get to this part in the line, then God will truly love me," or "When this happens, then I will have arrived." However, God paints in circles and not lines, so this is why at any point in your life He can touch the end and the beginning at the same time. He says, "I am the Alpha and the Omega, the First and the Last, the Beginning and the End" (Rev. 22:13). Any point He touches in your life, He is at both the mess and the message, the test and the testimony. This is good news, folks, because God is not waiting for you to arrive to see the greatness He has painted in your life. You are already an amazing work of art created by God. No matter how dark the moment is, darkness only lasts for the night because the morning is coming. You are complete in Christ Jesus; this knowledge will make you fearless. I'll leave you with this Scripture:

> *For those God foreknew he also predestined to be conformed to the image of his Son, that he might be the firstborn among many brothers and sisters. And those he predestined, he also called; those he called, he also justified; those he justified, he also glorified. What, then, shall we say in response to this? If God is for us, who can be against us?* [Romans 8:29–31].

NOTE

1. KIS KIS - keep it short, "CG Short film 'The Present' - by Jacob Frey ** Award winning **," May 23, 2019, YouTube video, https://www.youtube.com/watch?v=WfxQuD9weWM.

ARE YOU A SAUL OR DAVID?

CHAPTER

13

Jesus shows the depths of His forgiveness when after being betrayed and hung on the cross, He says, "Father forgive them" (Luke 23:34). Let me clarify something about forgiving others. Forgiveness doesn't mean they didn't hurt you. Forgiveness is deciding that you don't want to live with their hurt any longer. It's saying to the one who hurt you, "You no longer get to live rent-free in my mind." For me, I have always had an easy time forgiving because I know that God is the judge. As long as we try to wear the judge uniform, God is absent from the courtroom. There are so many times when I have forgiven because I think, *This is awesome! God, now You can get them. I'm out of the way.*

This type of thinking isn't how Jesus went about forgiveness, though. Jesus wrecks me when I read, "Father, forgive them, for they do not know what they are doing" (Luke 23:34). This is the type of forgiveness we need to walk in. This level of forgiveness says, "God, would You turn Your head on what they have done? Would You overlook this offense?" When we can forgive like that, we will experience true freedom.

We all have "Sauls" who have hurt us or rejected us. However, not forgiving your Saul will make you become just like him. I remember one day years ago, standing in the bathroom, staring into a mirror with tears welling up, asking God why He allowed Sauls into my life. I asked Him, "Where are the fathers that will push the next generation ahead?" I'll never forget how He answered. He said, "Jeremy, you're asking Me the wrong question. You keep talking to Me about Saul. What you need to be asking Me is not why you're facing a Saul, but who has become your David." "What do You mean, God? I am David," I responded. Well, God had a different perspective on what was happening. He said, "Whatever you don't forgive, you become, and you have become a Saul to a David in your life." It hit me like a ton of bricks. *I would never do something like that to someone else,* I thought to myself. Then, I realized that all the Sauls in my life were just Davids that never released Saul. They started protecting themselves, putting up walls, thinking they were locking Saul in, keeping Saul out, but the prison became their own. When you don't feel great, you can't allow anyone around you to be great. Your life is given to your own self-preservation instead of pushing the next generation forward. I was wrecked with this revelation. I had a David, and he felt like me. I was the one he despised. He was the one who would cry out to God, asking the same questions I was asking: "God, why would you put a Saul in my life?" I began to weep uncontrollably, asking God to show me my Davids. The Lord put an incredible young man on my heart, someone whose ideas I had shut down many times before because I needed to make sure my own were heard. The next time I saw him, I told him what the Lord had spoken to me, and to my surprise, he began to weep, telling me that I was indeed his Saul.

I learned something that day: my job is not to control those who hurt me, but only to control how long I let their hurt live within me. This will not be easy, the pain of their attack hurts so deeply because attack comes usually from someone close, maybe a friend, a mentor, a parent, a sibling, or a child. David says it this way in Psalm 55:12–14:

> *If an enemy were insulting me, I could endure it; if a foe were rising against me, I could hide. But it is you, a man*

like myself, my companion, my close friend, with whom I once enjoyed sweet fellowship at the house of God, as we walked with the worshipers.

> MY JOB IS NOT TO CONTROL THOSE WHO HURT ME, BUT ONLY TO CONTROL HOW LONG I LET THEIR HURT LIVE WITHIN ME.

When the arrow hit you, it took you by surprise. Both shocked and confused, you became a recluse because of the pain. I've found that we tend to leave the arrow in, continuing to suffer from the wound. The initial puncture hurt so badly that we did not have the power to deal with the pain of removing it. Instead, we decide to leave the arrow where it is, thinking we will be better off doing so. We say to ourselves, "At least the pain is over for now."

When you live with the arrow stuck inside you, you still have something to hold against them. I mean, they did this to you. They put you here. They are the problem, right? Well, the downside of living with your arrows is that no one can get close to you. Every time they walk forward, you take two steps back. If they get too close, they will bump one of the arrows, and you will be in agony all over again.

Have you ever bumped someone's arrow? Maybe you said something or forgot to say something. Maybe you forgot to call or text back, and out of nowhere, they flew off the handle. Shocked by their anger, you just wrote them off as strange, a little crazy, or maybe just emotional. It wasn't any of those things, though. You just bumped an arrow. You can bump someone's arrow when you look like someone they used to know who hurt them. Or maybe their arrow is bumped by certain genders, or by father or mother figures. Many times, those who have been wounded by pastors or churches will write you off, or not allow you in just because you associate with Jesus. Your connection to Jesus or to church bumps their arrows. The devil's greatest ploy is to not only shoot the arrow in us, but to get us to leave the arrows there, allowing life to heal the places around the wound, while not truly healing the wound itself. The hurt we don't deal with doesn't just affect our relationships with other people, though. It affects our relationship with God. Have you ever felt offended with God? Sometimes, we feel hurt, upset, or disappointed with God because of our faulty perceptions of who He is, or what He has done or not done, and we distance ourselves from Him. Keeping others, especially God, at a distance, is no way to live. If I want to get close to God and to the men and women of God in my life again, I have to begin to remove the hurt, the abuse, and the wounds of the past, one by one. If not, every time people get too close, I have to push them away.

David was simply bumping Saul's arrows, and Saul was shooting at David to keep him from getting too close. What the enemy doesn't want you to do is to take the arrows that have been hurled at you and use them as your weapons against him. He threw spears and arrows at you through the hurt he caused in others, but no matter how much he threw at you, he couldn't kill you.

Do you know the point at which your story becomes powerful? It's when you allow your wound to become a scar. A scar still has the memory, but without the pain attached. There was indeed pain, but now the pain is gone. Now, it's not just a story of "I'm hurting," but it's a story that declares, "I used to be hurt, and now I've been healed." An unhealed wound says, "I know what it's like to hurt," but a scar says, "I know what it's like to hurt, but I also know what it's like to be healed." It is in this place of allowing God to heal our wounds that He can use our lives greatly to bring healing to others.

Forgiveness is free for the offender, but costly for the one forgiving. However, the cost of unforgiveness has no limit. Let's press on like Jesus, always choosing to forgive and love again. Let it be said of us as it was of Him in 1 Peter 2:23:

> *When they hurled their insults at him, he did not retaliate; when he suffered, he made no threats. Instead, he entrusted himself to him who judges justly.*

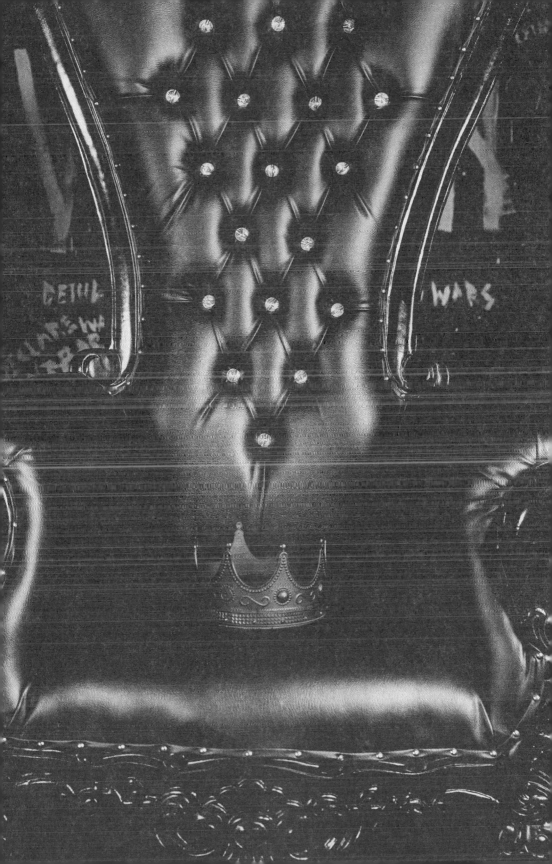

DIVINE
DETOUR

DIVINE DETOUR

CHAPTER 14

When we make everything about Him, our lives become supernatural. Our dreams and our families are His, and He always takes care of what is His. Church planting has been no different. Planting a church in a major metropolitan area was all new to Christy and me. There were a lot of things I didn't think about before the journey. Some things were impossible to know; some I didn't know just because of a lack of maturity. As I look back, hindsight is always 20/20. A venue was one of the major things that was shaky when Fearless started. Coming from being a youth pastor, my mind wasn't thinking about needing a venue because we had just used the church. Now, I see how blessed we were to have a building to meet in. Some might look at the places we have had the opportunity to meet and say, "That must be awesome," like scoping out someone's Instagram highlights without knowing how many low moments they had along the way, or how many failed selfies they took that they never posted. Although it was awesome that so many clubs opened their doors to us, they came with a few negatives. One of the main issues was they could only have us for two or three weeks at a time because of the constant demand for venues in our city. From award show after-parties, to birthday parties, to the launch of a new fashion line, there were all sorts of events in these venues. So, when Fearless started, we had around five different homes. From Hollywood, downtown, Westwood, and Silver Lake, we bounced from club to club. We even met in places as diverse as an Armenian television studio, Charlie Chaplin Studios, various theaters, and J.B.'s favorite nightclub. Really, we'd meet anywhere someone would host us and was within our budget. Most of my early days were spent

touring different venues. Sometimes, we didn't know where we were going to be the next week. Many times, at the end of the service we would announce, "Check Instagram midweek to find out where we're going to be next week."

Another thing I didn't foresee moving to LA was the cost to rent venues. When I looked at most church-planting websites' budget examples, they were built for small towns using a high school or theater. We lived in the movie/entertainment capital of the world. People made a living off of renting out their spaces to films and events. Obviously, this skyrocketed the prices, and we found ourselves constantly trying to talk people down from their lofty charges. Often, we would find a venue we loved, and then, last minute, it wouldn't work out, so we'd scurry to find a venue that could host us. Week to week, we relied on social media to help us spread the word about our Sunday location, and it worked. Sometimes, we would move and end up drawing more people, as if maybe people wanted to check out the new venue. Over time, though, as you can probably imagine, it got really old. We longed for a place we could call home, even if it was just our home on Sundays.

One particular week, the Fearless BND and I were on a trip in Florida. I was speaking at an event, and the band was leading worship for the weekend. Christy and I had decided to take the whole family with us since she was leading worship and I was preaching. It was me, Christy, my daughter, and my newborn son all packed into a room together. Our family got an opportunity to go to Disneyworld the day before the event, and while we were there, we got an unexpected phone call. The venue we had booked for Sunday was canceling on us. Apparently, it was some famous actor's birthday, and it was going to be financially better for the club to rent to them than to us. I immediately started to stress out. I mean, what were we supposed to tell people? It was Friday! To start looking for a new venue for that Sunday while being on the other side of the United States seemed impossible. I can remember being in the most wonderful place in the world with the best people in the world, just sick to my stomach and filled with stress all day. Then, I heard the voice of God say, "Jeremy, whose church is this?" What an incredible question. God has a way of asking us questions that change our perspective. I had forgotten that this Fearless thing wasn't my church. I was a worker with God, but not the boss. He is the one who is in charge of His church. I remember being in Disney looking up at the sky and saying, "God, You're right. This is not my church; it's Yours; This is Your battle, not mine." A weight was lifted off my shoulders, and for the rest the day I enjoyed Disneyworld with my family.

The next morning, as I got ready to speak at the event, I had a voicemail from one of the clubs we had reached out to. In fact, this was the first club I had found in LA. For whatever reason, it never worked out for us to be there—the pricing, permits, etc. The woman on the voicemail expressed her excitement to have us on Sunday. She said, "I've heard great things about Fearless." I put the phone down and realized in that moment, this really wasn't my church. Every moment I'm stressing out, I'm carrying what only He was meant to carry. Well, we ministered at the event and the next day flew back to LA, drove straight to service, arriving just minutes before the set-up team began. It was another incredible day at Fearless; people got saved, and God moved. We were all buzzing at how cool the new venue was. It was right in the heart of downtown LA, and even the workers were kind to us. That was unusual, believe it or not. During the middle of a service at one club we rented, two employees at the venue got into a fistfight in the sound booth. We later found out both of them were drunk. I will say this, though, one of the guys was actually trying to protect the church from the other guy. Then, there were these giant LED balls throughout the room, hooked to the ceiling that just kept moving up and down and changing colors during the oddest times during the service. Later, we found out this was not a part of the light show, but a drunk worker trying to sabotage our service. All of that to say, when we went to this new venue and experienced a venue staff that seemed almost excited that we were there, it was amazing, and that exuberance consumed the atmosphere.

The next week, we went back to venue hunting and bouncing from place to place. We would've loved to stay at Exchange LA, but their rate, although discounted, was way above our budget. A few weeks went by, and I kept getting calls from a random LA number a couple times a week, but every time they called, I was too busy to answer. After a few tries, the number finally left a voicemail. It was Angela from Exchange LA. Her tone was kind, but she said, "You are the hardest guy to get a hold of! I've been calling and calling. Call me please." I felt bad that I hadn't been answering, and now I was nervous to call her back. I knew she wanted us to rent her venue again, and believe me, we wanted to rent the venue, but I knew that we couldn't afford it. Honestly, I was a little embarrassed that their low price was too high for us.

Reluctantly, I called her back, and boy, was I shocked to hear what came next. Angela told me a story about her boss and how he had an encounter with God on the night we came to Exchange LA. She explained that he was in his home office, and he and his wife were in a fight over something dumb from earlier that night. He logged onto his computer and started checking emails, leading him down the email trail about our church renting the venue that night. He popped onto their online video feed in the main auditorium where I was speaking. He said as he listened to me preach, he felt peace come over his house. Then he heard a voice that said, "Go tell your wife sorry." I always say this is the first modern miracle of our church—a husband telling his wife sorry. Come on, we know that's a rare occurrence.

After that moment, he was consumed, checking out more videos from our church, our website, and our podcasts. Every week in their staff meeting he would ask Angela to get a hold of us and bring us back to Exchange LA. He'd say things like, "I want them here every week. They will bring peace to our nightclub." As Angela told me the story, I was shocked, and then my heart got sad again because I knew we couldn't afford to rent this club every week. I told Angela, "Thank you so much! What kind words. We're so thankful your owner would want us there." Then, I finally let the cat out of the bag. "We can't afford it! I know that you brought the price way down. I know the price is amazing for what you get, and people would jump at it in this city, but Angela, we're a church plant. Our budget is extremely small. Thank you for your offer, but we just can't afford it." Angela interrupted me in the middle of my statement, "Well, tell me what you can afford; it doesn't hurt to ask. The owners seemed to like you guys a lot." I told her the price that was within our budget, and I think I heard her giggle a little bit. She said, "I'll ask; it can't hurt to ask, right?" Within thirty minutes, Angela called me back saying, "You're never going to believe this; he wants to do it! Not only that, but if you want to store your stuff in our basement, we are open to that. We want you here every week; that is, if you guys want to be here."

All of a sudden, the last three months made sense to me for the first time. There was no way I would have appreciated that moment if I had not been through what I had been through. It happened in the moment I thought God had forgotten us. I had grabbed ahold of the wheel of the ship because I thought this Captain, God, was an absent Captain when we needed Him most. *I'll have to drive us through this storm,* I thought. I had it totally wrong; it was the Captain who allowed the storm so we would find His faithfulness in a new way. If the other venues had never canceled on us, we would have never found our home. I'm learning in life that when things get crazy, the best first response is to ask God what He's up to. We've been at Exchange LA ever since. I've also had several opportunities to go to lunch with the owners of Exchange LA. It's interesting because they're not your typical club owners. They are just businessmen who happen to run a nightclub. In fact, they were some of the first to come into downtown LA, which was a mess when they arrived. They pioneered a movement of businesses that would come into the city. When they started, it was a ghost town, abandoned by all for warmer waters, or should I say, the nicer areas in the city. Now, I realize that God wasn't just giving us a building. He was giving me access to these two men's hearts. During our time together at lunch, they told me that they had just been voted the "Number One Nightclub in the Nation" at a nightclub award show they went to in Vegas. One of the owners said, "So you know why we got this award? We got it because Fearless is in our nightclub. We're Potiphar, you're Joseph. You're our good luck charm." It was funny that he mentioned that because a few months before we met up, I began to notice things changing at the nightclub. When we first started renting the club, there was a Buddha statue that stood about 7 feet tall, placed behind where I preach, overlooking the dance floor. Around the room there were 10 prominent figures and famous philosophers painted, people who have been worshipped around the world—Gandhi, Mohammed, and others. Each one was about 5 feet tall. In the green room, where I would prepare before service, there were 150 masks on the walls, and those things were creepy. Slowly, over time, these things started disappearing. The owners realized that Jesus was all they needed in their business. They didn't need all the other religious figures around anymore. It's amazing what God can do in any environment. Light always kicks out darkness, and truth always destroys hate. God has always had you and will always lead you. You're in the palm of His hand; trust His process. Sometimes the palm of His hand can be the darkest spot. You may feel surrounded, but remember you're always surrounded by Him.

About 12 times a year, Exchange LA will ask us to move to a new venue for whatever reason. Usually it's because a large event has been booked on a Sunday. It could be American Idol auditions, a Lil Jon concert, the BET Awards, you name it. Since we have a handshake-type deal and because of our relationship, we often find another venue without any questions so that the club doesn't have to turn down events because of us. In turn, we meet new faces and experience new spaces. We bounce back and forth between clubs and event centers, and we have even met in an Armenian television studio, a Mexican food restaurant, and a CrossFit gym. The location doesn't really matter to us, as long as we can turn up and bring the Gospel to LA.

GOD HAS ALWAYS HAD YOU AND WILL ALWAYS LEAD YOU.

Supperclub was one of the venues we ended up renting on one of those Sundays. This home for the day was unique because it was a nightclub with beds. Yeah, you read that right. There were beds everywhere instead of seats. The theme was all about having supper in bed. People would lie down in a bed together, eat hors d'oeuvres, and watch a burlesque show, while dancers repelled from the ceiling on ropes. It was definitely one of the most unique places we'd ever brought the Gospel. This may be offensive to many that we would host church services in a place like this, but I believe this is the exact type of place Jesus would be. We've always had a strong belief that we were called to bring the light and love of Jesus into dark places. Los Angeles has some dark places, but this was one of the top, directly off Hollywood Boulevard, next to a smoke shop and a strip club.

Since there were beds we couldn't get rid of, I thought, *I'll just preach from the story in the Bible when the man was lowered through the roof on a bed.* What a day it was!

We were right on the main strip, so we invited many guests who were passing by on Hollywood Boulevard, people from all over the world. Tons of people came into the church that day who may have never entered a church otherwise. One person we ministered to that day was the owner of the nightclub. We hadn't heard until later that evening, but he was under an eviction notice. The week before we arrived, the police shut down his nightclub because of prostitution, illicit drugs, and the many other things that go along with those two activities. Everything he had poured his heart into was now gone. He was coming out of his office during the sermons and services, peeking in to see. As each service passed, he became more and more joyful. When we first got there, I imagine he probably thought to himself, *Well, it's money, so be kind.* By the end of the day, though, his kindness had become genuine; you could tell! During our last service, some police officers threatened to shut us down because the club was no longer supposed to operating. We told them we were a church, but it took them a while to believe me. At this point, we were only just learning of all the things that happened in this nightclub. Then, the police officer started telling the owner, "This is a good idea. We need some more church going on in dark places like this." Later that evening, I found the same police officer inviting several people passing on the street into our service.

We had agreed to be at Supperclub for two weeks, so during the week after the first Sunday, I asked the owner if

I could take him to lunch to hear his story and more about the nightclub. As I was driving to lunch, I had no clue what we would talk about or even why I had planned this lunch in the first place, other than to reach another lost person in our city. I believe the owner went to lunch with me because he thought I was going to offer to buy his lease from him in the building that he could no longer use. On my way there I began asking God, "What would You have me say to this man?" Then, Jesus gave me a vision right as I was on Interstate 405. It was so vivid that I felt like I was there. I saw the man in a giant house with all of his furniture covered in plastic. The house looked like it wasn't being lived in, and I saw him in the middle of a giant bed, all alone, with his face pushed into a high-end silk pillow, screaming out over and over, "I want to die! I want to die! I want to die!" This was a strange vision because the guy I met on Sunday seemed pretty happy, like he had it all together.

I got to lunch, and after some small talk, I had the impression from the Lord to tell him the vision. So eventually, when the time was right, I shared with him what I felt God showed me. He was really awkwardly quiet after I shared. Then he began to speak. "How did you know?" I responded, "I didn't, but I believe someone heard you. You see, it was God who was listening to what you thought was a private conversation with yourself. Sir, we weren't moved from Exchange LA for no reason." I don't believe it was the party that was booked at Exchange that moved us; it was God rerouting us so He could go after the one. I said, "Sir, I didn't hear you that day, but God did, and He sent me to tell you that He loves you and He longs to be close to you." I explained salvation and how Jesus came and died on a cross for our sins. I shared how the cross wasn't the end, but that on the third day He rose back to life, and how just like Jesus rose to life, He wants to give us new life. Right there in the middle of the restaurant, that nightclub owner gave his heart to Jesus. After we prayed, the man jumped up in the middle of the restaurant and said, "I feel alive." I said, "That's what Jesus does. He alone brings dead people to life." He responded, "So what do I do now?" "What do you mean? What you do now is live life. Do what you've always done, but just do it for God." Instantly he got on the phone and started inviting people to church the next week. He said, "Now, I won't invite people to the club; I'll invite them to the house of God." That day I learned a huge lesson. There is always more than what you see, more than what you know; God is always up to something. You never know what God is up to, so what looks like an accident or mistake could end up being powerful if you ask God to let you in on His purpose in it. Keep your eyes and ears open; today's problem could be God's hand positioning you for great things.

GOD IS ALWAYS UP TO SOMETHING.

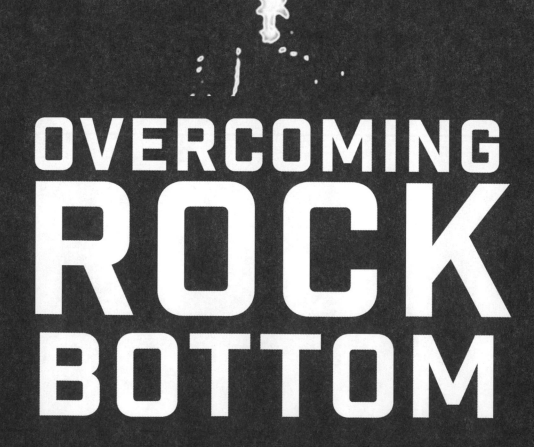

OVERCOMING ROCK BOTTOM

OVERCOMING

ROCK

BOTTOM

15

CHAPTER

Crashing quickly and totally burned out, I knew something was wrong when at 3:00 a.m. I was hunched over the hotel toilet throwing up blood, and I could not remember what city I was in to preach this time. When I was 17 years old, I said yes to following Jesus, and from that moment, I had gone hard after the call to bring life to dead people. The only problem was that I forgot that I, too, was just a human being, stuck in a body with physical limitations. My health had gotten so bad over time from the time spent on the battlefront. I reached the point where I thought sleeplessness was just a part of my DNA.

Now, as I sit writing this book seven months after that moment, it has taken this long for me to just begin to understand how I got there and that I would have to learn how to do life in a new way. I still am unraveling the wrong theologies and lies I bought into, both about myself and God and how I believed God saw me. I laugh now looking back at some of the things that, not even seven months ago, I took great pride in and preached with unwavering passion. I will never see those things the same way again. One of the lies I believed went something like this: "I will sleep when I die." Yes, it's true that we will rest when we die, but in the context of life on earth, it's not quite how we were designed to live. However, that's exactly what was happening to me. I was slowly dying from the inside out.

What I learned in these last seven months will be so valuable to me in making it for the long haul in ministry. I used to believe that God was pushing me this hard and He had given me the passion, so I had to push like I did. Since then, I've found out that much of the passion I burned with was not biblical at all;

it was a way for me to prove to myself and others that I wasn't failing. Once I returned home from the trip, I got on a phone call with one of my mentors. It wasn't just that night of being sick in the hotel room that alarmed me. It was that something had shifted in me. Things that didn't used to irritate me now bothered me greatly. Fears I thought I had defeated were at an all-time high, including the fear of flying, particularly, landing. After experiencing a few rough landings, every time the pilot said, "Get ready for landing," my heart rate would speed up. I would start sweating, thinking thoughts like, *What are my kids going to end up like 30 years from now without a dad?* I knew these thoughts were not from the Lord; I just didn't know why I had grown so vulnerable to fear's bark when I once ruled over it.

Here I am, the pastor of Fearless LA, and yet I'm losing the battle to fear a second time. Seven years ago, fear was broken off my life, including the fear of flying, which was something I would be called to do. Since that moment, I can't tell you how many planes I've been on without any fear or anxiety. Many of those flights were peaceful and enjoyable. I had never known what it was like to actually enjoy living the life God gave me until fear was silenced in my life—at least I thought it was silenced. Now, fear's voice had come back for round two, and it seemed like fear was winning the fight. I felt like Rocky at the end of the seventh round, limping, bloody, bruised, and hoping to knock out this foe that seemed to escape my every swing.

Swing after swing, fear was winning the fight. After a few close encounters with what felt like death, it seemed impossible to get gloom and doom out of my head. The truth of the Word grew quiet amidst the loud facts of my circumstances. I was embarrassed that I had gone backward, that I felt so sick, so tired, and so worn out. To top it all off, for the first time in my life I was actually working out. Besides those days in high school, I had been far too busy to hit the gym. But for the last few months, I'd been a part of a CrossFit gym. I could run farther and jump higher than ever before, but for some reason my body was beginning to break down. It seemed like every time I did CrossFit, I got worse. I'd get some pain in a random organ. In fact, the pains I had moved throughout my body. One month, it was my stomach. The next month, it was headaches that lasted for two months. Then came the worst of them all—I had the symptoms of a heart attack that lasted three months. During those three months, I went to the ER five times, three of them by myself.

My wife started to get tired of my expensive trips to the ER, each time finding out that I was not actually having a heart attack. Fear can manifest itself in real physical symptoms, and stress works its permanent damage in our bodies. I learned that Google was not my friend. In the middle of the night, I was left to read articles about the worst-case scenarios of what was going on in my body. It seemed like afterward I would read about some sickness or pain, or see a late-night commercial about something, and I would end up with the same symptoms. They always came in the middle of the night, when I was left alone to my own thoughts. This kept me from the real thing I needed—rest.

What a patient and good Father we have. When I was at my worst, God sent me doctors along the way to encourage me. Even though they found nothing wrong, it was like I was sitting at an altar call moment at the end of our visit. Many times, instead of making me feel stupid for coming in, the doctor would try to help me find rest from the fear that was causing the anxiety. One doctor in particular kicked the nurse out of the room and gave me three extra tests to prove to me that I was not having a heart attack. After the tests turned up negative, he rolled his stool next to my bed and began to minister to me. He told me his story. While studying to be a doctor, this exact thing happened to him. He would get anxious, his heart would begin racing, and all the symptoms that he had studied would flood his mind. He got to the point where he quit college, quit going to movies, quit dating, and would just sit in his room. Now, years later, I was his patient dealing with the same thing. As I sat there, I began to weep, releasing all the fear and confusion. I felt like for the first time someone understood me.

All that time, I was still trucking along, posting to Instagram like everything was great. To the outside world, my life was awesome, the church was doing well, and my family was happy, but truthfully, I was broken. At a conference, I met another pastor who had gone through the same thing. He shared with me about his journey back to freedom. It felt like he was reading my mail. He explained something called adrenal fatigue, and although I didn't fully understand it, I knew I was experiencing the same symptoms. After that conversation, I thought, *Well, I can't stop traveling. This is my call. I can't make a lot of the changes he did when he was sick.*

With a trip to Korea scheduled the next day, I boarded the plane as planned and headed to the next conference. I made a promise to myself that I would speak up for myself and tell the host of the conferences and churches that I would only be able to be in my session, and then I would need to rest during the other portions of the day. I thought this might help, or at least be some sort of a step in the right direction. Boy, was I wrong. In Korea, not only was I alone in a new country, but my body began to break down even more. I would just lose my voice, and the anxiety was overwhelming, plus I had a long flight to endure.

When I got home, I called a mentor, who since then has become like a spiritual father. I described what I had been walking through to him for the first time. He started to see where I was really at. My thought processes were so off that I thought taking a break at a conference was going to be the fix to this 15-year journey of brokenness in my body, soul, and spirit. I was so wrong. Thank God he was in my life to call me out on it. I don't think I would be writing this book if he hadn't. Right away, he said, "We've got to get you help. I'm committed to you for the long haul." He asked me to get him in contact with my wife, and he was going to meet with her to put together a plan on how to get me better. They got together, and their plan was pretty intense to me. They wanted me to take 30 days off from everything— cancel the next 30 days of travel, let my wife, Christy, run the church and staff, and I would simply be a dad and rest. When the kids were at school, I would have an opportunity to work on myself and figure out what it was that was ultimately causing me all this pain—physically, spiritually, and mentally.

I was scared out of my mind, but we went forward with the process. People that were expecting me to come speak were very understanding. We met with the church, and everyone unanimously got behind us. I think it's somewhat because they had seen so many pastors in their past burn out, and they didn't want that for me. They raised money that day in church so that Christy and I could live without traveling. The best advice I was given at the start was that this sabbatical's purpose was for me to find myself again. It was so that I could remember that I was a human with needs, likes, and desires.

When the 30 days began, I bought myself a sewing machine, went to thrift stores, got a record player, and visited the beach. I began the journey of trying to find myself again as a son, a human, or not God's robot or warrior. I began to discover how He made me. Who was Jeremy the person, not Jeremy the preacher? I found out why I liked the things I liked and disliked the things I disliked. I didn't really know exactly what I was supposed to do to find myself again. Every day I woke up and asked the same questions: "What's wrong with me?" and "Who am I?"

About two weeks in, I had made three jackets, painted a couple of pictures, and had a new tan from the beach. However, I was no better than when I started. I was still full of the same fears. In fact, some of the pains in my body had gotten worse. I got ahold of my mentor again and began to lay out where I was in this 30-day journey. Here I was, 15 days in, and I felt like I hadn't even started the journey to wholeness. It felt like I was on mile one of a 1,000-mile race to find myself again. During the conversation, he interrupted me and said, "Jeremy, it's not 30 days." For some reason, the thought of 30 days had put a new stress on me. I had this unrealistic expectation that I only had 30 days to fix myself, like a deadline on a calendar before all hell broke loose again. I had been caught up in the rat race for so long that even in a time of rest, I was throwing myself back into the cage.

He said "Jeremy, it's as long as it takes; 30 days was just the beginning. Stop thinking about the 30 days and start asking God, 'How do I begin?'" Something shifted that day, and my mind started breaking free from the feeling of forced change, to learning how to walk it out day by day. At some point during the break, I ended up at my parents' house. There is something about going back to your roots that reminds you of who you are and how far you've come since the days you walked those high school hallways. On the drive back to Los Angeles, I got a call from a friend who had heard what I was going through and desperately wanted to speak to me. He left a voicemail, so I called him back. It was so good to hear a familiar voice from a great friend. It was even greater to hear that he also had walked through the very same thing that I was now walking through. The only difference was that he was a couple of months ahead in his journey toward wholeness.

He began to describe to me in more depth about adrenal fatigue and leaky gut syndrome, two things that are caused by stress in an adrenaline-junkie atmosphere like the one I had created for myself over the last 15 years. After saying yes to Jesus, I just went for it. Nothing else mattered. It's almost like I forgot that I was in a body. My spirit was alive, and it seemed my body no longer mattered. He laid out to me how I would have to walk and live in order to recover. So, I took his advice. I started going to bed on time, eating the right foods, paused CrossFit, stopped doing anything competitive, and did everything in my own time. This was a unique lifestyle change for me.

Through the diet and lifestyle changes, I began to see substantial changes. I was no longer waking up in the middle of the night with weird pains in my body. Once I removed the toxins, my body just began to heal itself. It took rest, a very strict diet, and the right type of exercise. Beyond this, my mentor wanted me to dig deeper than just fixing the physical stuff. He wanted me to look at the spiritual side of things to find out what had put me in this place where I felt like I had to work myself so hard, to find out what it was that made me work myself to the point of sickness for the Lord. He set up an appointment for me to have a Sozo session at the Transformation Center in Redding, California, which is connected to Bethel Church. I had no clue what to expect. What was it that needed to be dug up from the graveyard of past mistakes, hurts, and wrong thinking? Being a pastor is my greatest love, but the wounds of others along the journey had been almost fatal to me.

The church in Redding was amazing; it was everything you would expect from Bethel Church. The power of God was flowing freely. Something I noticed in extreme measures was the amount of peace that surrounded the campus. When Monday morning came, I met with my counselor, Darrell, and to my surprise, it was much different than I had expected. I have been in a lot of deliverance sessions. I have even performed many of them myself, but never once had I experienced anything quite like what I experienced there. We got to the Transformation Center, and it did not look like a church at all, but rather, a doctor's office. It was located in the middle of a shopping center.

In the front room, there were a few chairs with magazines at hand's reach, and a window where you fill out your form to let them know what's going on in your body and your life. When I got to the room, it was small, and Darrell was an elderly man with a kind smile. First, he told me his testimony; before he gave his life to Jesus, he lived in LA and was an atheist. God came into his life and rescued him, and he moved to Redding to join the internship at Bethel at the ripe age of 50. Now 20 years later, he was counseling others, using what he had learned along the way.

He opened our time up by explaining Sozo ministry, the theology behind it, and how it works. Sozo ministry was the process they had developed to walk people through inner healing. He explained that in Sozo, they typically found that the issues that we carry as adults usually stem from moments that took place before the age of five. These moments impact us so deeply because they happen when we're forming what we will believe for the rest of our lives about the world. They determine how we interact with the world and how it interacts with us. He said that we are impacted the most by our fathers. We are both nurtured and destroyed by what our fathers do, whether they show us love or fail to.

Shortly after, Darrell began to ask me questions about my dad. I quickly responded that I had an incredible dad. I mean, even to this day he texts me every couple of days to let me know he is praying for me, and he usually tags a quote or Scripture to encourage me. He also is still married to my mom, and they seem happier now than ever before. If Darrell was going to try to find my problem there, it wasn't going to happen. In fact, when we moved to Los Angeles, my mom and dad decided to move with us and help us plant the church. They left their home in the country with 60 acres, their friends, and their lives to move into a trailer they owned. They set up their trailer in a mobile home park in Orange County. From there, they went on to run our kids' ministry for the next three years. My dad was a legend of a dad, from whom I got inspiration from on a daily basis for raising my kids. My greatest aspiration is to one day be half the dad he has been. We all have our issues, but there was nothing that my dad could have done that would have caused this fraction in my relationship with God.

Darryl persisted, though. "Let me just ask you a few questions, and let's see what God does." After about five questions that didn't seem to get us anywhere, Darrell asked me a question that will ring through my head for the rest of time. He said, "Finish this statement for me: 'I wish my dad would have...'" At first, nothing came to me, as we had our eyes closed in the small room. Out of nowhere, the words came out: "I wish my dad would've taught me." I didn't fully know what that meant until Darrell began to prod a little more. He said, "Let's ask Father God what that means." When I asked Him, immediately I had a vision. It was me as a five-year-old on the front lawn of the house I grew up in. My dad and I were in the front yard with a brand-new football we had just bought at the local hardware store. We were throwing the football back and forth; neither of us was very good. It looked like I was trying to learn how to throw and catch. About the fifth catch in, my dad's shoulder began to hurt from an injury that happened at his work. On top of the pain, he wasn't really skilled at throwing the ball. I didn't know then, but I realize now that he was embarrassed that he couldn't throw the ball to me very well or teach me how to catch it.

When he was a kid, he was a farmer. He grew up milking cows from sunup to sundown. He was an expert at many things, but sports was not one of them. He knew everything there was to know about saddling a horse and taking care of farm animals, but when it came to sports, my dad was like a fish out of water. In my vision, he almost threw as bad as me at five years old. As I was playing catch with him, something shifted. He said "Son, my arm's hurting too bad. I don't think that I'm going to be able to teach you how to throw or catch. If you want to learn this, you'll have to teach yourself." He walked away and went to mow the lawn and take care of the house. The vision ended with me throwing the ball into the air and trying to catch it alone in the front yard.

As I explained it to Darrell, a sudden flood of emotions began to take over. I don't remember all that happened after that, but I cried throughout the remainder of the meeting. I realized that I had bought into a lie. From that moment until now I had lived that lie as truth. The lie that if I was going to learn anything in life, that I was going to have to teach myself, and that is exactly what I did. I knew nothing about football, but for the next 10 years I studied every aspect of it. In fact, when I started high school football, it took me all the way until my senior year to be able to start on the team. I worked out three times a day, trying to prove that I could do it. The problem was I was the smallest on the team, constantly getting hurt, but getting back up. Even my high school newspaper wrote a story about me, almost like I was the local Rudy.

If you know the story of Rudy from Notre Dame, he went from being a walk-on to playing in a real-life game. With that same mentality, I had succeeded at everything I ever put my mind to. My mentality was that at the end of the day, if I pushed hard enough, worked long enough, I would ultimately get to where I wanted to go. Some of us would call that good work ethic. For many years of my life, I had deemed this as a great attribute about myself, and I thought God was proud of me for it. I thought I was reflecting parts of who He was through those qualities in me. I was so wrong. It wasn't my work ethic that drove me so hard; it was the lie that I had believed that became true to me. I believed that if I ever was going to learn something, nobody else would teach me; I would have to teach myself. Then, Darrell made the statement, "However you see your dad is how you see Father God." When I heard those words, the reality of life and its truth hit me so hard that I cried for the next hour. Emotion flooded in like a dam that had been broken over a city.

> WHEN YOU'RE RUNNING WITH GOD, THERE IS GRACE AND PROTECTION. WHEN YOU'RE ON YOUR OWN PATH, EVEN DOING A GOOD THING, THERE IS NO PROTECTION; THERE IS NO COMFORT; THERE IS NO PEACE.

I thought God was like my dad, that He wanted to cheer me on and be proud of me, but at some point, He would walk off the field, too, and I would be left with the ball in my hand. Throughout life, I subconsciously believed that God was saying, "Son, I want you to do it, but you'll have to do it alone. I won't be able to teach you." I knew God was for me; I knew He loved me. What I didn't know was that He doesn't just call me into things; He guides me through them. I realized that God wanted to teach me all things—how to be the pastor of Fearless Church, a father to my children, a husband to my wife, and how to discover and use the gifts He gave me. He would even show me how to walk through the hurt and pain of those who rejected or left me.

I realized that for the last 15 years, I had been running in front of God, not with Him. That's a dangerous place to be because when you're running with God, there is grace and protection. When you're on your own path, even doing a good thing, there is no protection; there is no comfort; there is no peace. I needed to learn to rest in the fact that ultimately, every call was God's call. I would need to learn that as I walked with Him, He would teach me along the journey, and He would never leave me nor forsake me.

In my first meeting with Darrell, I received several weapons that I would use in my fight against the enemy's lies that would come over the next few months. For the first time in a long time, I felt like I could breathe again. Several things came out of that meeting with Darrell. Number one: healthy people get counseling, not sick people. To this day, I still see Darrell once a month through FaceTime. Many times, before we get on the call, I have no clue what we will talk about until something happens during my day that will bring up another wound, another piece that I need to work through. It took me 15 years of ministry to get this way, and if you were to look at my life, I believed a lie for 33 years, so it might take a while to unravel that lie, even though I've been set free. That freedom is worth every second spent opening the puzzle box again and discovering new things that have been left out.

At the end of one of our sessions, I ended up crying again and learning something new about myself. Just when I thought I was healed, God reveals another wound under the armor. Darrell says it this way: "Well, we got another piece of the puzzle." It seems like this puzzle is one that takes a lifetime to put back together, with the only one that can—Jesus. In another session with Darrell, I learned I have the gift of prophetic feeling, which explained a lot of the pains and feelings that I was experiencing. I explained that I kept feeling an overwhelming sense of fear that I was going to die, leaving my kids without a dad and my wife without a husband. We started praying together, and we discovered that this thought came from the moment my uncle passed away from cancer. I distinctly remember that I didn't want to see him while he was fighting cancer. I was too nervous to go to the hospital and see him all hooked up to tubes, cancer eating away at his body. He had gotten so bad that he was on his deathbed. My parents encouraged me to go see him, knowing he didn't have much time left. I knew of others whose friend or family member had cancer, but this was the first time it hit so close to home. I finally agreed to go see him.

In tears, I began to describe this to my counselor, and the memories of the hospital room filled with the smell of death, the sound in his lungs as he struggled to breathe, the sunken look of his eyes, and the pale tone of his skin came back to me. It was as if I was reliving that painful moment all over again. I could only stay in the hospital room with him for two minutes, then I busted out of the room in tears. I ran until I ran out of breath and found myself as a 16-year-old kid in the middle a field, beating my hands on the ground, yelling at God. As I described the scene to my counselor, he interrupted me and said, "Jeremy, what I'm about to say to you is going to shock you. What you were feeling wasn't the spirit of fear, but the spirit of compassion." I did not understand at all how the fear I was feeling could be compassion. I pressed him a little. "Help me understand." He continued to minister to me, saying, "You were feeling fear that day, but the fear wasn't yours. It came from the others in the room. You have since believed a lie and have walked in it that whatever you feel is inside of you." He then blew my mind and made the statement again. "What you felt was fear, yes, but the fear you received wasn't yours. You came in that room with compassion and left with the fear that filled that room. Jeremy, God didn't give you fear that day; He gave you compassion."

Then, he asked me if I had ever heard of the term "prophetic feeler." It sounded like a cool ability one of the X-Men had, but I had never heard of it. He described the gift of prophecy and how it worked. Some people are hearers; they hear God say something, then act on what they hear. Some are seers; they see something from God, then act on what they see, like dreams, visions, and the like. Others are feelers; they feel something in the spirit, and then act on that. He said, "Jeremy, you may have seen and you may have heard, but there is a third area you have been operating in with what you feel in a room. Because you didn't know this existed or was a way God speaks, you have taken on everything you feel as your own." In that moment, I had a sudden shift in my countenance. My life began to flash before my eyes. This whole time, I had thought all these feelings were mine. Many times, I felt like I was going crazy. I was angry, alone, depressed, and in pain, only to discover that God had been speaking to me all along. I learned that I was able to pick up on environments, sensing people's feelings down to the pain they felt, both emotionally and physically. That afternoon, I began reading everything I could get my hands on about this, scouring the internet for others who had experienced this, too. My mind was blown away discovering more about this gift God had given me. For so many years, it seemed like a curse. I was both overwhelmed and excited about what God was showing me.

PROPHETIC FEELINGS

There is more to you than you know; it's not always managing the stuff that is negative, but we must also manage our gifts. For a significant portion of my life, I had denied that I could be a prophetic voice, confusing the office of the prophet with the gift of prophecy. Although we are not all appointed to the office of prophet, all are called and have the opportunity to flow in the gift of prophecy. It's just as all aren't called to the office of a pastor, yet we are all called to preach the Gospel. Our call is ultimately to be vessels that contain God Himself, and because we cannot contain Him, we live in a state of overflow. This overflow can come in the form of healing, serving, prophesying, and the like. Prophecy couldn't have been introduced any clearer than when Peter preached his first sermon echoing the prophet Joel in Acts 2:17 (KJV), "And it shall come to pass in the last days, saith God, I will pour out of my Spirit upon all flesh: and your sons and your daughters shall prophesy."

> OUR CALL IS ULTIMATELY TO BE VESSELS THAT CONTAIN GOD HIMSELF, AND BECAUSE WE CANNOT CONTAIN HIM, WE LIVE IN A STATE OF OVERFLOW.

We are those that Peter spoke of in his sermon. We are currently living in those last days. How cool is it that there is no qualification other than being a son or a daughter? What's even more amazing is that God pours Himself onto us, not some other thing from heaven, but Himself. Lastly, He doesn't create a class system to determine how much we can receive. In other words, there are no Happy Meal-sized portions in the King-dom of God. He only has one size—supersize. It's for the one-day-old Christian and the 20-year veteran. He promises it to all. So why is it that only a small portion of God's kids walk in this gift? Many reasons come to mind, but for me, it was a lack of understanding.

There are three ways people flow in the prophetic gift, and all of them bring life to the world around them. There are those that see, those that hear, and those that feel. Those that see will often get pictures of what God is saying. Those that hear will often hear a spoken word or command from God, which could be audible or through a resonating voice inside their hearts. The final way in which God speaks is through feelings and emotions.

I knew that God could speak through words or pictures, but it set me free when I had the revelation that God could also speak through my feelings. I have since learned because of this gift I am sensitive to environments. Not only can I feel the heart of God for things, but I can feel the emotions of the people in the environments that I walk into. Before I had this revelation, I would think that all the feelings I was having were mine. As you can imagine, living in a crazy city like Los Angeles can make one feel like they are going crazy. Not only this, but flying all the time doesn't add more peace to the mixture.

Thankfully, I've learned that not all of the feelings I have while walking the city streets or flying from one place to the next are mine. For example, sometimes I'll step onto a plane with full confidence and assurance that God is going to keep me safe. Then, sometime during the flight, the plane will go through a bump of turbulence, and all of a sudden fear comes, along with emotions contrary to what I had previously. I used to think it was me, and I would try to solve what I was feeling from that perspective. Then, I realized that if I'm a prophetic feeler, these feelings I'm experiencing could be from the people around me. I also discovered that I could feel people's physical pain, and many times if I'm not careful, that pain can cause me to think something is going on in my body. Just as I can feel someone's anger and mistake it for my anger, I can feel someone's pain and mistake it for my own. Since coming to an understanding of this for myself, I have been able to have another option for every feeling or pain I receive. Instead of automatically assuming it's mine, I first think about if it could be coming from the environment around me.

At first, this was overwhelming not knowing what to do with all the stuff I was reading. At the same time, it was freeing to know it was something I couldn't turn off, and that just because I felt it, didn't mean that I was expected to change it. God didn't always want me to do something with it just because I felt it. I now have learned to ask God when feeling something in the atmosphere, "What do You want me to do with this, Father?" If God tells me to do nothing, I recognize those aren't my feelings or pains and leave them there. If He wants me to do something, He makes it clear to me.

Recently, I was in New Zealand, and I had a crazy pain in my left backside for the entire day before I preached. The old Jeremy would have had no other option but to think the pain was his own. I'd be searching on Google for the answer and imagining all the worst-case scenarios. However, with a new understanding of this gift, I asked God, "Is this mine or someone else's?" Immediately, I heard God tell me that I was going to pray for someone that night with this pain, and they were going to get healed. While I was preaching, I described the pain I was experiencing. When it started, where it was, and the level of pain. Sure enough, out of 700 young adults, one girl in the very back shot her hand up in the air. We prayed, and the pain in her backside miraculously left, and so did mine.

All prophetic seers, hearers, and feelers are different. The gift of prophecy can manifest in different ways. This gift, like most gifts God gives, will take a lifetime to unwrap. At 38 years old, I feel like I'm just now beginning to understand this thing. The prophetic is something a person can grow in upon discovery. It isn't an automatic growth, but something we come to know through the Word and through practice. As we go through the process of sharpening this gift, we will become better stewards of it. We're also not limited to only one prophetic gift; we can walk in all three in different moments. God wants to give all of His children good gifts, so don't be shy. Ask Him!

THE PROPHETIC IS SOMETHING A PERSON CAN GROW IN UPON DISCOVERY. IT ISN'T AN AUTOMATIC GROWTH, BUT SOMETHING WE COME TO KNOW THROUGH THE WORD AND THROUGH PRACTICE.

OBEDIENCE IS SUCESS

OBEDIENC

IS

SKESS

16

Success in the call of God can only be found in obedience. Many times, when someone has fallen off the horse of their purpose, we see their passion for God dwindle. We often ask: "Have you been spending time with God?" or "How has your time with God been?" Although this sounds good, I have found it's not only spending time with God that fuels us in the Kingdom. It's not only about knowing that His name is powerful or being in His presence, although those things are important. Even the demons shudder at His name. What will fuel us is in our decision to follow Him wholeheartedly.

Both Judas and Peter walked with Jesus. Both the woman with the issue of blood and the crowd around her were near Him. The ones who followed Him to death and the ones who denied Him both experienced the presence of Jesus. However, they received two different fates. The only difference I see in Peter, the woman, and His followers who were with Him until death compared to the others was their heart for obedience. They valued His will and His opinion over their own. While one was picking up his rights, the other was laying them down. Make sure you lay yours down.

Many people have walked with Jesus while walking out their dream, thinking the two are the same, while all along delaying, or ultimately, destroying their destiny. Many have been in His presence, but not in His will. They've been near Him, but not letting Him near the real them. So the question isn't if you're spending time with Him, if you've encountered Him, or even if you are walking with Him. The question is this: Have you turned over your life to Him?

> *You are my friends if you do what I command* (John 15:14).

Does the Lord delight in burnt offerings and sacrifices as much as in obeying the Lord? To obey is better than sacrifice....Because you have rejected the word of the Lord, he has rejected you as king (1 Samuel 15:22-23).

Fear promises us that as long as we take control of our lives, we will never have to get hurt again. Well, if you have been alive and breathing very long, you know that even if you are in control, you still have opportunities to get hurt, maybe even daily. One realization that changed my perspective was this: Kingdom success is putting God in control. Once He is in control, fear has to go. My daily prayer is for God to reveal to me His perspective of success in every situation. I'm not a failure when I'm not in control. The world has its own definition of success, but I know that I have true success when I place God in control, even when everything feels out of control. God is faithful. Now, when we go through difficult times, our prayer becomes, "God, how are You going to help me through this moment?" First Corinthians 10:13 tells us that when we are tempted, He will provide a way of escape so that we can endure it. His promise to us is not that we won't go through troubles or feel tempted to quit. He promises that He will give us what we need to endure them. He tells us in John 16:33 that we will have many troubles in this life, but to take heart because He has overcome the world. Only He has the power to help us overcome. God has always been there, and He will always be there. We can trust Him to teach us how to live fearlessly in this world that is overtaken by fear.

Sometimes we want to walk in disobedience, take shortcuts, and still hold the blessing. When we do this, we become a Jacob generation, dressing up in Esau's clothes, putting fake fur on our skin to manipulate the Father's blessing. We say things like, "I left, but hey, I was blessed." We start dating a person even though there were red flags, saying, "Oh, don't worry; I got the blessing." You receiving the blessing through manipulation is you delaying the first thing God was trying to teach you: obedience. When you force the hand of the Father to bless you, you get the birthright but miss the power.

> WHEN YOU FORCE THE HAND OF THE FATHER TO BLESS YOU, YOU GET THE BIRTHRIGHT BUT MISS THE POWER.

Obedience teaches us to praise God even when we don't see His goodness. Your praise is a weapon not to just be healed from but also to war against. Today is the day of salvation. Let me say it this way, many times throughout my life I've been told that we are the Joshua generation. What does that mean and does it really help me? I found that something deep inside me resonated with Joshua and his generation. You see, Joshua's generation watched Moses's generation live steps from their promise and carry the Word with them, yet they never saw the word fulfilled in them. Joshua's generation had a different vision of who God was. Moses's generation waited until God won the victory. They got to the Red Sea, and as soon as they had a problem, they were ready to throw away their promise, and with that, their God seemed to all of a sudden have no power. Many of them even threw their hands up and said things like, "It'd be better to go back to where we started as slaves than to be free and be stuck." Then, God opened the sea, because even to the faithless He shows Himself faithful. They successfully passed through the Red Sea on dry land and came up on the other side. They watched their enemies wash up on shore after the sea's power had destroyed their enemy, and then they would praise. The Bible says that Miriam busted out her tambourine, and she sang an epic song because God did it again. But just moments earlier, God had "forgotten" them. This was not Joshua's generation. They were different. Somewhere in the desert they had learned, or maybe there was something inside of them that knew God is who He says He is. Maybe there was a fire inside of them that they couldn't contain or explain. Maybe there was a voice saying, "There has to be more than what I see with my eyes, God. If you're really God, you're always God."

The Joshua generation learned to praise on this side of their pain. It was at the wall, while the wall was still erected and huge, shouting in front of them, that they shouted back praises to our God, and the wall fell. God is raising up a generation that praises on this side of their problem, while it's still in front of them, not just after God does the miracle. I dare you to put down the book and experience God right there in your room as you worship. Maybe you're going through something difficult right now. Don't let the devil get the victory in the now. What if you chose to praise Him even if you don't see the breakthrough yet? Join with the Joshua generation who realized that praise was their weapon.

To all the warriors who say, "I know all of this. I've tried fearing God and knowing my Word in the battle, yet still I'm here at the same place I started." I say to you, "Try again." The enemy knows He can't defeat you, so he works overtime to wear you out in the fight. I can attest to this; I've been worn out many times by my battle with fear. Recently, my perspective shifted while I was studying for a sermon about the age-old story of David and Goliath. As I was reading the text, I saw something different that gave me new hope: David was not called on by God to merely fight Goliath; he was called to kill Goliath, to destroy him completely. These are two very different ways of looking at the story. I've always looked at the story and thought, *What is my Goliath that I'm called to fight?* I saw it as something I'd have to battle my whole life, as something I'd have to really focus on. When I read the story this time, though, I saw that this was not the top of the mountain for David; it wasn't the end. David battling and defeating Goliath was just a stepping stone to the next thing God had called him to: becoming the king.

When I refer to Goliath, he represents the thing that meets you when you wake up in the morning and the thing that robs your sleep at night. It's not a "here today gone tomorrow" type of problem. It's something you've dealt with for a while. In the Scripture, Goliath was there for 40 days and 40 nights taunting the army of God. For me, my Goliath was fear, and as I read this story again, it shocked me to realize that David didn't just fight Goliath; he killed Goliath. There was a day that Goliath was no longer breathing. He was no longer living. He could no longer taunt or throw his insults David's way. What does this mean for you? You are called to win, and winning doesn't just mean battling something; it means totally defeating it. This is good news for us. This means we can live in freedom in a way we have never experienced if we do not give up.

Where have you stopped? Is there something you believed that you would fight your whole life? Now's the time to stand up to that lie and to defeat Goliath. What stood on the other side of David defeating Goliath, not simply sparring with him, was a powerful call to be king. I'm telling you today that whatever is on the other side of your greatest fear is greater than your fear itself. It was worth David fighting and conquering Goliath to be able to step into kingship. It is worth it for you to face your Goliath and defeat him. Don't give up at "I'm just an anxious person." Don't give up at "I'll always be afraid" or "I'll always deal with this." You are not your Goliath. There is more for you. You were called to face this fearlessly.

Again, the concept of being fearless is found in the word itself. It's two words: *fear* and *less.* The goal is to fear less than yesterday. We have adopted a statement at Fearless: "Love more, fear less." Believe me, though, just because this is our mission, doesn't mean I have arrived and have this all figured out. Every day I'm just taking another step toward love, and when I do, I'm taking a step away from fear. Fear is something that I am still battling. I remembered this David and Goliath illustration in the middle of the night while I was having night terrors about something I was going to do the next day. So, it's not that fear is fully destroyed in me, yet; it's that God gave me a mindset shift in the middle of the battle that helped me take another step forward. My prayer for this book is that you experience the same mindset shift to help you continue moving forward every day. Each step you take, you are closer to defeating that ugly giant.

> *Let us not become weary in doing good, for at the proper time we will reap a harvest if we do not give up* [Galatians 6:9].

The key words in the verse above are "do not give up." Thomas A. Edison once said, "Our greatest weakness lies in giving up. The most certain way to succeed is always to try just one more time."

That's why you dream one more time, believe one more time, hope one more time, and love one more time. Life is full of ups and downs, many things that bring great joy or incredible heartache. One thing that remains consistent is pain; Jesus Himself told us we would have trouble (John 16:33). However, He empowers us in the second part of the verse, saying, "But take heart! I have overcome the world." It is because He overcame that we can determine to overcome. It's the stories of those who have overcome that move us, not just those that have made it to their goal. We want to see people who not only have made it to, but those that have made it through.

I love the music of Beethoven, but I am moved even more by it when I know the story of the man behind the music. Ludwig van Beethoven

- masterfully played the violin for 5 years,
- was an accomplished pianist for 13 years,
- studied under Mozart for 20 years,
- wrote many symphonies,
- began losing his hearing at the age of 20, and
- was completely deaf by the age of 50.

He was determined to get his music out even after he was deaf. He sawed off the legs of his piano and laid on the floor with it so he could feel the vibrations of his music. He wrote his greatest symphony without the ability to hear, through sheer determination.

> YOUR GREATNESS DOES NOT LIE IN THE FACT THAT YOU DO WHAT YOU DO, BUT MORE SO IN THE FACT THAT YOU SHOULDN'T BE ABLE TO DO IT.

I want to suggest to you that grace is opposed to earning, but not to effort. While pounding his piano, Beethoven said, "I will take fate by the throat; it will never bend me completely to its will." This is the kind of passion we need to get back in our lives again. The kind of passion that says, "I have already won, and I am determined to remind life and this world that no matter what it throws at me, I'm going to keep going." The unique thing is that his music was amazing before he lost his hearing, but it went to another level after he lost his ability to hear. It's not just remarkable because he made music that changed the world; it's remarkable because he shouldn't have been able to make music at all. He was determined to never let his world defeat or change him. Similarly, your greatness does not lie in the fact that you do what you do, but more so in the fact that you shouldn't be able to do it.

MANAGEMENT OR A MIRACLE

We go to God for many things in life. We cry out for a miracle, ask Him to heal a damaged relationship, or to get us out of health or financial issues, but what we really need is not only a miracle, but management. On the other side of the spectrum, sometimes we try to manage only, when the only thing that will do is a miracle. I have gone through seasons pursuing one side, when really I should've been pursuing the other. Some are asking for a financial miracle, but God might be saying, "Stop spending more than you make. Set up a budget, surround yourself with people who are good with finances, start tithing (10 percent of your income), give offerings (above and beyond your tithe)." God is saying, "You don't need a miracle, you need management. Walk out My principles, and provision will come." Maybe you're walking through some health issues and praying for Him to make you healthy, but just be ready. Depending on what's going on, God might say, "You need to stop smoking, you need to stop eating horrible food, and you need to exercise." God could give you a miracle, and I believe He wants to, but the miracle is not found in God's doing, but rather in our partnership with what God has revealed to us in the Word. Sometimes it's found in our management.

Let's take it a step further. Look at what Hebrews says to those in this race of faith:

> *Therefore, since we are surrounded by such a great cloud of witnesses, let us throw off everything that hinders and the sin that so easily entangles. And let us run with perseverance the race marked out for us, fixing our eyes on Jesus, the pioneer and perfecter of faith. For the joy set before him endured the cross, scorning its shame, and sat down at the right hand of the throne of God* (Hebrews 12:1–2).

Did you see that? Let us throw off everything that hinders us. Then, He uses the words "and the sin." I point that out because it is clear that there are some things that will slow us down or hinder us that aren't sin. Our dreams, pursuits, and will at times can hinder us from real power that is found in our position. Again, there can be good things that aren't God things. The Bible is clear that it's our job to throw these off in order to reach God's purposes. The only way we will have the power to do that is to keep our eyes on Jesus, pursue love, and defeat fear, embracing a truly fearless life.

You have been set apart by God, and for that reason you must switch your fear. You have been chosen to change your world. What God has given you is enough to walk in your destiny. God sees you and loves you. You're not abandoned. All the strength you need in this battle called life is Him as your source. Being planted in His house, gives life to your purpose. Prayer will always be better than worry. God is in the business of transforming lives; He is the Master of broken pieces. He wants to lead you to discover your identity in Him, forgiving your enemies. In Him there is nothing you can't conquer? Fear has no chance!

> *No king is saved by the size of his army; no warrior escapes by his great strength* (Psalm 33:16).

No matter how mighty you are, you cannot deliver yourself. Only God can save you from fear's power. Your job is to put yourself in a position to be delivered by God. Being obedient, renewing your mind with identity in Christ, refusing to agree with fear, renouncing fear's lies, standing on the Word of God, and speaking the Word out loud over yourself create a position of deliverance for God to fill. Proximity to God is where you get His weapons against the spirit of fear. Just as some doors only open with proximity, the door to freedom opens the closer you align yourself with His Word over you.

> *For God hath not given us the spirit of fear; but of power, and of love, and of a sound mind* [2 Timothy 1:7 KJV].

You have to be close to hear it from God. There is a big difference between reading the Bible and hearing it from the author. Faith is needed to defeat fear. It's my prayer like the disciples', "Lord, increase our faith." Our faith is increased when we receive His word from the author.

> *So then faith comes by hearing, and hearing by the word of God* [Romans 10:17 NKJV].

Word here is *rhēma*, which is the spoken Word of God. Faith grows and fear shrinks when we hear the Word of God from God Himself. When the Father gives a Scripture to His children, it becomes real to them. Fear is the antithesis of faith. We can say it like this: fear is simply having faith in the devil or receiving rhema from the devil. Just like God has a word over you, so does the devil. You must decide which one to listen to. Just like faith is having confidence in and trusting God, fear is having confidence in the enemy and trusting his lies. The reason why you are afraid is because you believe that what you are afraid of will come to pass. For instance, if you are afraid of failure, that means you believe in failure; if you are afraid of losing money, that means you believe in losing money. Fear is a spirit, and God has not given us the spirit of fear, but He has given us the spirit of love, power, and a sound mind to overcome fear. Over and over, the Bible repeats "Fear not!" or "Have no fear!" or "Do not be afraid!" or "Be not afraid!" God did not do that on accident; He was giving you ammunition for your fight. It's time to stop ignoring fear and declare war on it!

Declare these words out loud every day on your battlefield. Fear's power over you ends here! Take the throne back; take back your crown; open your mouth and declare and denounce fear and watch fear run. By faith claim your fearless life today!

I declare this battle over.

I give my fear to God.

I can trust in You.

I will not fear because I am Yours and You take care of what's Yours.

You call me by name.

You will never leave nor forsake me.

Nothing can separate me from You.

I will not give into anxiety about anything; I'll talk to You about everything.

Your peace surrounds me and guards me.

When I get in trouble, You're my deliverer.

You are with me.

I can do hard things because You're my strength.

I will not fear.

I have power and authority to overcome all.

Nothing will harm me.

It's my faith that extinguishes all the arrows of the enemy.

You strengthen me when I don't believe.

You are my shield and great reward.

You have given me weapons that are powerful.

I take all my thoughts captive.

You strengthen me and protect me.

You give grace when I need it.

In your love I never have to fear.

You take care of all my needs.

Your Word is my food and gives me life.

I submit to You and the enemy runs.

I set my heart on things above.

You will finish what You start.

You help me to trust You.

Thank You for love. power, and a sound mind.

You are my strength and what I sing about.

I choose today to be strong and courageous, no more trembling for You are with me.

I will not give way to panic.

Lord, You are the one who fights for me.

You give victory.

The battle is not mine but Yours, God.

The only fear I will embrace is fear of You.

When I fear You, who is left to fear—no one.

I give no room to worry or anger.

You have my back.

I commit myself to You.

These declarations are based on the mighty and powerful Word of God:

> Cast all your anxiety on him because he cares for you (1 Peter 5:7).

> When I am afraid, I put my trust in you. In God, whose word I praise—in God I trust and am not afraid. What can mere mortals do to me? (Psalm 56:3–4)

I have redeemed you; I have summoned you by name; you are mine (Isaiah 43:1).

I will never leave you nor forsake you (Hebrews 13:5 NKJV).

For I am convinced that neither death nor life, neither angels nor demons, neither the present nor the future, nor any powers, neither height nor depth, nor anything else in all creation, will be able to separate us from the love of God that is in Christ Jesus our Lord (Romans 8:38-39).

Do not be anxious about anything, but in every situation, by prayer and petition, with thanksgiving, present your requests to God. And the peace of God, which transcends all understanding, will guard your hearts and your minds in Christ Jesus (Philippians 4:6–7).

I sought the Lord, and he answered me; he delivered me from all my fears (Psalm 34:4).

I can do all things through him who gives me strength (Philippians 4:13).

So do not fear, for I am with you; do not be dismayed, for I am your God. I will strengthen you and help you; I will uphold you with my righteous right hand (Isaiah 41:10).

I have been given authority to trample on snakes and scorpions and to overcome all the power of the enemy; nothing will harm you (Luke 10:19).

Take up the shield of faith, with which you can extinguish all the flaming arrows of the evil one (Ephesians 6:16).

I do believe; help my unbelief! (Mark 9:24 NASB)

Do not be afraid....I am your shield, your very great reward (Genesis 15:1).

The weapons we fight with are not the weapons of the world. On the contrary, they have divine power to demolish strongholds (2 Corinthians 10:4).

We take captive every thought to make it obedient to Christ (2 Corinthians 10:5).

The Lord is faithful, and he will strengthen you and protect you from the evil one (2 Thessalonians 3:3).

Grace and peace be yours in abundance through the knowledge of God and of Jesus our Lord (2 Peter 1:2).

There is no fear in love. But perfect love drives out fear, because fear has to do with punishment. The one who fears is not made perfect in love (1 John 4:18).

My God will meet all your needs according to the riches of his glory in Christ Jesus (Philippians 4:19).

Whoever looks intently into the perfect law that gives freedom, and continues in it—not forgetting what they have heard, but doing it—they will be blessed in what they do (James 1:25).

Submit yourselves, then, to God. Resist the devil, and he will flee from you (James 4:7).

Set your hearts on things above, where Christ is, seated at the right hand of God (Colossians 3:1).

He who began a good work in you will carry it on to completion until the day of Christ Jesus (Philippians 1:6).

You will keep in perfect peace those whose minds are steadfast, because they trust you (Isaiah 26:3).

For God has not given us a spirit of fear, but of power and of love and a sound mind (2 Timothy 1:7 NKJV).

I will fear no evil, for you are with me (Psalm 23:4).

Don't be afraid; just believe (Mark 5:36).

Surely God is my salvation; I will trust and not be afraid. The Lord, the Lord himself, is my strength and my defense; he has become my salvation (Isaiah 12:2).

For I am the Lord your God who takes hold of your right hand and says to you, Do not fear; I will help you (Isaiah 41:13).

Do not fear the reproach of mere mortals or be terrified by their insults. For the moth will eat them up like a garment; the worm will devour them like wool. But my righteousness will last forever, my salvation through all generations (Isaiah 51:7–8).

Be strong and courageous. Do not be afraid; do not be discouraged, for the Lord your God will be with you wherever you go (Joshua 1:9).

Be strong and courageous. Do not be afraid or terrified because of them, for the Lord your God goes with you; he will never leave you nor forsake you (Deuteronomy 31:6).

Do not be terrified; do not be afraid of them. The Lord your God who is going before you, will fight for you, as he did in Egypt (Deuteronomy 1:29–30).

Today you are going into battle against your enemies. Do not be fainthearted or afraid; do not panic or be terrified by them. For the Lord your God is the one who goes with you to fight for you against your enemies to give you victory (Deuteronomy 20:3-4).

Do not be afraid or discouraged because of this vast army. For the battle is not yours, but God's (2 Chronicles 20:15).

Blessed are those who fear the Lord, who find great delight in his commands....They will have no fear of bad news; their hearts are steadfast, trusting in the Lord. Their hearts are secure, they will have no fear; in the end they will look in triumph on their foes (Psalm 112:1,7-8).

To fear the Lord is to hate evil; I hate pride and arrogance, evil behavior and perverse speech (Proverbs 8:13).

The Lord is my light and my salvation, whom shall I fear? The LORD is the stronghold of my life, of whom shall I be afraid? (Psalm 27:1)

Be still before the Lord and wait patiently for him; do not fret when people succeed in their ways, when they carry out their wicked schemes. Refrain from anger and turn from wrath; do not fret—it leads only to evil. For those who are evil will be destroyed, but those who hope in the Lord will inherit the land (Psalm 37:7-9).

Do you want to be free from fear of the one in authority? Then do what is right and you will be commended (Romans 13:3).

if you devote your heart to him and stretch out your hands to him, if you put away the sin that is in your hand and allow no evil to dwell in your tent, then, free of fault, you will lift up your face; you will stand firm and without fear [Job 11:13–15].

Whoever listens to [wisdom] will live in safety and be at ease, without fear of harm [Proverbs 1:33].

Fear of man will prove to be a snare, but whoever trusts in the Lord is kept safe [Proverbs 29:25].

Search me, God, and know my heart; test me and know my anxious thoughts. See if there is any offensive way in me, and lead me in the way everlasting [Psalm 139:23–24].

Whoever dwells in the shelter of the Most High will rest in the shadow of the Almighty. I will say of the Lord, "He is my refuge and my fortress, my God, in whom I trust." Surely he will save me from the fowler's snare and from the deadly pestilence. He will cover me with his feathers, and under his wings you will find refuge; his faithfulness will be your shield and rampart. You will not fear the terror of night, nor the arrow that flies by day, nor the pestilence that stalks in the darkness, nor the plague that destroys at midday [Psalm 91:1–6].

When I said, "My foot is slipping," your unfailing love Lord, held me up. When anxiety was great within me, your consolation brought me joy [Psalm 94:18–19].

Do not let wisdom and understanding out of your sight, preserve sound judgment and discretion; they will be life for you, an ornament to grace your neck. Then you will go on your way in safety, and your foot will not stumble. When you lie down, you will not be afraid; when you lie down, your sleep will be sweet [Proverbs 3:21–24].

You may say to yourselves, "These nations are stronger than we are. How can we drive them out?" But do not be afraid of them; remember well what the Lord your God did to Pharaoh and to all Egypt. You saw with your own eyes the great trials, the signs and wonders, the mighty hand and outstretched arm, with which the Lord your God brought you out. The Lord your God will do the same to all the peoples you now fear....Do not be terrified by them, for the Lord your God, who is among you, is a great and awesome God" (Deuteronomy 7:17–19, 21).

Do not be afraid. God has come to test you, so that fear of God will be with you to keep you from sinning (Exodus 20:20).

When one rules over people in righteousness, when he rules in the fear of God, he is like the light of morning at sunrise on a cloudless morning, like the brightness after rain that brings grass from the earth (2 Samuel 23:3–4).

Let the beloved of the Lord rest secure in him, for he shields him all day long, and the one the Lord loves rests between his shoulders (Deuteronomy 33:12).

"Don't be afraid," the prophet answered. "Those who are with us are more than those who are with them."... "Open his eyes, Lord, so that he may see!" (2 Kings 6:16–17)

Don't be afraid of them. Remember the Lord, who is great and awesome, and fight for your families, your sons and your daughters, your wives and your homes (Nehemiah 4:14–15).

As important as is it for you to declare the truth of God's Word, it's also vital that you denounce the enemy and his power over your life. We see Hannah do this when she prayed, "My heart rejoices in the Lord; my horn is exalted high because of the Lord. I have loudly denounce my enemies. Indeed I rejoice in your deliverance" (New English Translation).

To denounce is defined as "to take a public stand against something and make clear you don't like or are condemning it."[1] It's time to take a public stand against fear to condemn it. Repeat this out loud over your life:

I denounce the spirit of fear over my mind. You do not get to live in me anymore. I denounce fear over my future, fear from my past, and fear in the present. Fear, you must take your grip off my heart. I will live free from anxiety. I choose joy not depression, worship not worry. God holds tomorrow in His hands, so I will not fear tomorrow. I will live a fearless life, in Jesus's name.

NOTE

1. Yourdictionary.com, s.v. "denounce," accessed September 12, 2022, https://www.yourdictionary.com/search/result?q=denouce.

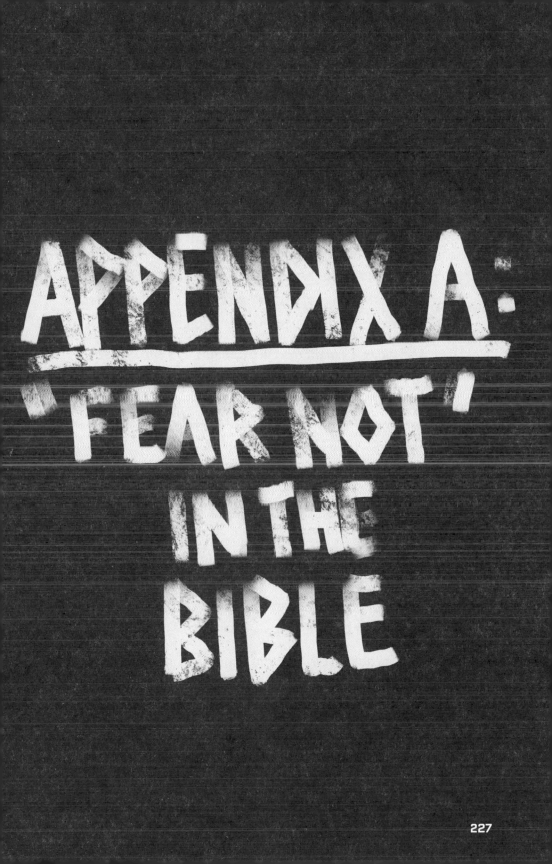

APPENDIX A:
"FEAR NOT"
IN THE
BIBLE

All verses in the Appendix A are from the NRSV.

TORAH/PENTATEUCH

After these things the word of the Lord came to Abram in a vision, "Do not be afraid, Abram, I am your shield; your reward shall be very great" [Genesis 15:1].

And God heard the voice of the boy; and the angel of God called to Hagar from heaven, and said to her, "What troubles you, Hagar? Do not be afraid; for God has heard the voice of the boy where he is" [Genesis 21:17].

And that very night the Lord appeared to him and said, "I am the God of your father Abraham; do not be afraid, for I am with you and will bless you and make your offspring numerous for my servant Abraham's sake" [Genesis 26:24].

When she was in her difficult labor, the midwife said to her, "Do not be afraid; for now you will have another son" [Genesis 35:17].

He replied, "Rest assured, do not be afraid; your God and the God of your father must have put treasure in your sacks for you; I received your money." Then he brought Simeon out to them [Genesis 43:23].

Then he said, "I am God, the God of your father; do not be afraid to go down to Egypt, for I will make of you a great nation there" [Genesis 46:3].

But Joseph said to them, "Do not be afraid! Am I in the place of God?" [Genesis 50:19]

"So have no fear; I myself will provide for you and your little ones." In this way he reassured them, speaking kindly to them (Genesis 50:21).

But Moses said to the people, "Do not be afraid, stand firm, and see the deliverance that the Lord will accomplish for you today; for the Egyptians whom you see today you shall never see again" [Exodus 14:13].

Moses said to the people, "Do not be afraid; for God has come only to test you and to put the fear of him upon you so that you do not sin" [Exodus 20:20].

And I will grant peace in the land, and you shall lie down, and no one shall make you afraid; I will remove dangerous animals from the land, and no sword shall go through your land [Leviticus 26:6].

Only, do not rebel against the Lord; and do not fear the people of the land, for they are no more than bread for us; their protection is removed from them, and the Lord is with us; do not fear them [Numbers 14:9].

But the Lord said to Moses, "Do not be afraid of him; for I have given him into your hand, with all his people, and all his land. You shall do to him as you did to King Sihon of the Amorites, who ruled in Heshbon" [Numbers 21:34].

You must not be partial in judging: hear out the small and the great alike; you shall not be intimidated by anyone, for the judgment is God's. Any case that is too hard for you, bring to me, and I will hear it [Deuteronomy 1:17].

See, the Lord your God has given the land to you; go up, take possession, as the LORD, the God of your ancestors, has promised you; do not fear or be dismayed (Deuteronomy 1:21).

I said to you, "Have no dread or fear of them" (Deuteronomy 1:29).

The Lord said to me, "Do not fear him, for I have handed him over to you, along with his people and his land. Do to him as you did to King Sihon of the Amorites, who reigned in Heshbon" (Deuteronomy 3:2).

Do not fear them, for it is the Lord your God who fights for you (Deuteronomy 3:22).

Do not be afraid of them. Just remember what the Lord your God did to Pharaoh and to all Egypt (Deuteronomy 7:18).

When you go out to war against your enemies, and see horses and chariots, an army larger than your own, you shall not be afraid of them; for the Lord your God is with you, who brought you up from the land of Egypt (Deuteronomy 20:1).

The priest...shall say to them: "Hear, O Israel! Today you are drawing near to do battle against your enemies. Do not lose heart, or be afraid, or panic, or be in dread of them" (Deuteronomy 20:2–3).

Be strong and bold; have no fear or dread of them, because it is the LORD your God who goes with you; he will not fail you or forsake you (Deuteronomy 31:6).

It is the Lord who goes before you. He will be with you; he will not fail you or forsake you. Do not fear or be dismayed (Deuteronomy 31:8).

HISTORICAL BOOKS

I hereby command you: Be strong and courageous; do not be frightened or dismayed, for the Lord your God is with you wherever you go [Joshua 1:9].

Then the Lord said to Joshua, "Do not fear or be dismayed; take all the fighting men with you, and go up now to Ai. See, I have handed over to you the king of Ai with his people, his city, and his land" [Joshua 8:1].

The Lord said to Joshua, "Do not fear them, for I have handed them over to you; not one of them shall stand before you" [Joshua 10:8].

And Joshua said to them, "Do not be afraid or dismayed; be strong and courageous; for thus the Lord will do to all the enemies against whom you fight" [Joshua 10:25].

And the Lord said to Joshua, "Do not be afraid of them, for tomorrow at this time I will hand over all of them, slain, to Israel; you shall hamstring their horses, and burn their chariots with fire" [Joshua 11:6].

Jael came out to meet Sisera, and said to him, "Turn aside, my lord, turn aside to me; have no fear." So he turned aside to her into the tent, and she covered him with a rug [Judges 4:18].

But the Lord said to him, "Peace be to you; do not fear, you shall not die" [Judges 6:23].

And now, my daughter, do not be afraid, I will do for you all that you ask, for all the assembly of my people know that you are a worthy woman [Ruth 3:11].

As she was about to die, the women attending her said to her, "Do not be afraid, for you have borne a son." But she did not answer or give heed [1 Samuel 4:20].

And Samuel said to the people, "Do not be afraid; you have done all this evil, yet do not turn aside from following the Lord, but serve the Lord with all your heart" [1 Samuel 12:20].

Stay with me, and do not be afraid; for the one who seeks my life seeks your life; you will be safe with me [1 Samuel 22:23].

He said to him, "Do not be afraid; for the hand of my father Saul shall not find you; you shall be king over Israel, and I shall be second to you; my father Saul also knows that this is so" [1 Samuel 23:17].

The king said to her, "Have no fear; what do you see?" The woman said to Saul, "I see a divine being coming up out of the ground" [1 Samuel 28:13].

David said to him, "Do not be afraid, for I will show you kindness for the sake of your father Jonathan; I will restore to you all the land of your grandfather Saul, and you yourself shall eat at my table always" [2 Samuel 9:7].

Then Absalom commanded his servants, "Watch when Amnon's heart is merry with wine, and when I say to you, 'Strike Amnon,' then kill him. Do not be afraid; have I not myself commanded you? Be courageous and valiant" [2 Samuel 13:28].

Elijah said to her, "Do not be afraid; go and do as you have said; but first make me a little cake of it and bring it to me, and afterwards make something for yourself and your son" (1 Kings 17:13).

Then the angel of the Lord said to Elijah, "Go down with him; do not be afraid of him." So he set out and went down with him to the king (2 Kings 1:15).

He replied, "Do not be afraid, for there are more with us than there are with them" (2 Kings 6:16).

Isaiah said to them, "Say to your master, 'Thus says the Lord: Do not be afraid because of the words that you have heard, with which the servants of the king of Assyria have reviled me'" (2 Kings 19:6).

Gedaliah swore to them and their men, saying, "Do not be afraid because of the Chaldean officials; live in the land, serve the king of Babylon, and it shall be well with you. (2 Kings 25:24).

Then you will prosper if you are careful to observe the statutes and the ordinances that the Lord commanded Moses for Israel. Be strong and of good courage. Do not be afraid or dismayed (1 Chronicles 22:13).

David said further to his son Solomon, "Be strong and of good courage, and act. Do not be afraid or dismayed; for the Lord God, my God, is with you. He will not fail you or forsake you, until all the work for the service of the house of the Lord is finished" (1 Chronicles 28:20).

He said, "Listen, all Judah and inhabitants of Jerusalem, and King Jehoshaphat: Thus says the Lord to you: 'Do not fear or be dismayed at this great multitude; for the battle is not yours but God's'" (2 Chronicles 20:15).

This battle is not for you to fight; take your position, stand still, and see the victory of the Lord on your behalf, O Judah and Jerusalem. Do not fear or be dismayed; tomorrow go out against them, and the Lord will be with you (2 Chronicles 20:17).

Be strong and of good courage. Do not be afraid or dismayed before the king of Assyria and all the horde that is with him; for there is one greater with us than with him (2 Chronicles 32:7).

After I looked these things over, I stood up and said to the nobles and the officials and the rest of the people, "Do not be afraid of them. Remember the Lord, who is great and awesome, and fight for your kin, your sons, your daughters, your wives, and your homes" (Nehemiah 4:14).

WISDOM BOOKS

You shall be hidden from the scourge of the tongue, and shall not fear destruction when it comes (Job 5:21).

Surely then you will lift up your face without blemish; you will be secure, and will not fear (Job 11:15).

Their houses are safe from fear, and no rod of God is upon them (Job 21:9).

No fear of me need terrify you; my pressure will not be heavy on you (Job 33:7).

It deals cruelly with its young, as if they were not its own; though its labor should be in vain, yet it has no fear (Job 39:16).

It laughs at fear, and is not dismayed; it does not turn back from the sword [Job 39:22].

I am not afraid of ten thousands of people who have set themselves against me all around [Psalm 3:6].

Even though I walk through the darkest valley, I fear no evil; for you are with me; your rod and your staff—they comfort me [Psalm 23:4].

The Lord is my light and my salvation; whom shall I fear? The Lord is the stronghold of my life; of whom shall I be afraid? [Psalm 27:1].

Though an army encamp against me, my heart shall not fear; though war rise up against me, yet I will be confident [Psalm 27:3].

Therefore we will not fear, though the earth should change, though the mountains shake in the heart of the sea [Psalm 46:2].

Do not be afraid when some become rich, when the wealth of their houses increases [Psalm 49:16].

O Most High, when I am afraid, I put my trust in you. In God, whose word I praise, in God I trust; I am not afraid; what can flesh do to me? [Psalm 56:2-4]

In God I trust; I am not afraid. What can a mere mortal do to me? [Psalm 56:11]

He led them in safety, so that they were not afraid; but the sea overwhelmed their enemies [Psalm 78:53].

You will not fear the terror of the night, or the arrow that flies by day [Psalm 91:5].

They are not afraid of evil tidings; their hearts are firm, secure in the Lord (Psalm 112:7).

Their hearts are steady, they will not be afraid; in the end they will look in triumph on their foes (Psalm 112:8).

With the Lord on my side I do not fear. What can mortals do to me? (Psalm 118:6)

If you sit down, you will not be afraid; when you lie down, your sleep will be sweet (Proverbs 3:24).

Do not be afraid of sudden panic, or of the storm that strikes the wicked (Proverbs 3:25).

She is not afraid for her household when it snows, for all her household are clothed in crimson (Proverbs 31:21).

A wooden beam firmly bonded into a building is not loosened by an earthquake; so the mind firmly resolved after due reflection will not be afraid in a crisis (Sirach 22:16).

PROPHETIC BOOKS

And say to him, Take heed, be quiet, do not fear, and do not let your heart be faint because of these two smoldering stumps of firebrands, because of the fierce anger of Rezin and Aram and the son of Remaliah" (Isaiah 7:4).

Do not call conspiracy all that this people calls conspiracy, and do not fear what it fears, or be in dread (Isaiah 8:12).

Therefore thus says the Lord God of hosts: O my people, who live in Zion, do not be afraid of the Assyrians when they beat you with a rod and lift up their staff against you as the Egyptians did (Isaiah 10:24).

Surely God is my salvation; I will trust, and will not be afraid, for the Lord God is my strength and my might; he has become my salvation [Isaiah 12:2].

Say to those who are of a fearful heart, "Be strong, do not fear! Here is your God. He will come with vengeance, with terrible recompense. He will come and save you" [Isaiah 35:4].

Isaiah said to them, "Say to your master, 'Thus says the Lord: Do not be afraid because of the words that you have heard, with which the servants of the king of Assyria have reviled me'" [Isaiah 37:6].

Get you up to a high mountain, O Zion, herald of good tidings; lift up your voice with strength, O Jerusalem, herald of good tidings, lift it up, do not fear; say to the cities of Judah, "Here is your God!" [Isaiah 40:9]

Do not fear, for I am with you, do not be afraid, for I am your God; I will strengthen you, I will help you, I will uphold you with my victorious right hand [Isaiah 41:10].

For I, the Lord your God, hold your right hand; it is I who say to you, "Do not fear, I will help you" [Isaiah 41:13].

Do not fear, you worm Jacob, you insect Israel! I will help you, says the Lord; your Redeemer is the Holy One of Israel [Isaiah 41:14].

But now thus says the Lord, he who created you, O Jacob, he who formed you, O Israel: Do not fear, for I have redeemed you; I have called you by name, you are mine [Isaiah 43:1].

Do not fear, for I am with you; I will bring your offspring from the east, and from the west I will gather you (Isaiah 43:5).

Thus says the Lord who made you, who formed you in the womb and will help you: Do not fear, O Jacob my servant, Jeshurun whom I have chosen (Isaiah 44:2).

Do not fear, or be afraid; have I not told you from of old and declared it? You are my witnesses! Is there any god besides me? There is no other rock; I know not one (Isaiah 44:8).

Listen to me, you who know righteousness, you people who have my teaching in your hearts; do not fear the reproach of others, and do not be dismayed when they revile you (Isaiah 51:7).

Do not fear, for you will not be ashamed; do not be discouraged, for you will not suffer disgrace; for you will forget the shame of your youth, and the disgrace of your widowhood you will remember no more (Isaiah 54:4).

In righteousness you shall be established; you shall be far from oppression, for you shall not fear; and from terror, for it shall not come near you (Isaiah 54:14).

Do not be afraid of them, for I am with you to deliver you, says the Lord (Jeremiah 1:8).

Their idols are like scarecrows in a cucumber field, and they cannot speak; they have to be carried, for they cannot walk. Do not be afraid of them, for they cannot do evil, nor is it in them to do good (Jeremiah 10:5).

They shall be like a tree planted by water, sending out its roots by the stream. It shall not fear when heat comes, and its leaves shall stay green; in the year of drought it is not anxious, and it does not cease to bear fruit (Jeremiah 17:8).

I will raise up shepherds over them who will shepherd them, and they shall not fear any longer, or be dismayed, nor shall any be missing, says the Lord (Jeremiah 23:4).

But as for you, have no fear, my servant Jacob, says the Lord, and do not be dismayed, O Israel; for I am going to save you from far away, and your offspring from the land of their captivity. Jacob shall return and have quiet and ease, and no one shall make him afraid (Jeremiah 30:10).

Gedaliah son of Ahikam son of Shaphan swore to them and their troops, saying, "Do not be afraid to serve the Chaldeans. Stay in the land and serve the king of Babylon, and it shall go well with you" (Jeremiah 40:9).

Do not be afraid of the king of Babylon, as you have been; do not be afraid of him, says the Lord, for I am with you, to save you and to rescue you from his hand (Jeremiah 42:11).

But as for you, have no fear, my servant Jacob, and do not be dismayed, O Israel; for I am going to save you from far away, and your offspring from the land of their captivity. Jacob shall return and have quiet and ease, and no one shall make him afraid (Jeremiah 46:27).

As for you, have no fear, my servant Jacob, says the Lord, for I am with you. I will make an end of all the nations among which I have banished you, but I will not make an end of you! I will chastise you in just measure, and I will by no means leave you unpunished (Jeremiah 46:28).

Do not be faint-hearted or fearful at the rumors heard in the land—one year one rumor comes, the next year another, rumors of violence in the land and of ruler against ruler (Jeremiah 51:46).

You came near when I called on you; you said, "Do not fear!" (Lamentations 3:57)

And you, O mortal, do not be afraid of them, and do not be afraid of their words, though briers and thorns surround you and you live among scorpions; do not be afraid of their words, and do not be dismayed at their looks, for they are a rebellious house (Ezekiel 2:6).

Like the hardest stone, harder than flint, I have made your forehead; do not fear them or be dismayed at their looks, for they are a rebellious house (Ezekiel 3:9).

He said to me, "Do not fear, Daniel, for from the first day that you set your mind to gain understanding and to humble yourself before your God, your words have been heard, and I have come because of your words" (Daniel 10:12).

He said, "Do not fear, greatly beloved, you are safe. Be strong and courageous!" When he spoke to me, I was strengthened and said, "Let my lord speak, for you have strengthened me" (Daniel 10:19).

Do not fear, O soil; be glad and rejoice, for the Lord has done great things! (Joel 2:21)

Do not fear, you animals of the field, for the pastures of the wilderness are green; the tree bears its fruit, the fig tree and vine give their full yield [Joel 2:22].

The Lord has taken away the judgements against you, he has turned away your enemies. The king of Israel, the Lord, is in your midst; you shall fear disaster no more [Zephaniah 3:15].

On that day it shall be said to Jerusalem: Do not fear, O Zion; do not let your hands grow weak [Zephaniah 3:16].

My spirit abides among you; do not fear [Haggai 2:5b].

Just as you have been a cursing among the nations, O house of Judah and house of Israel, so I will save you and you shall be a blessing. Do not be afraid, but let your hands be strong [Zechariah 8:13].

So again I have purposed in these days to do good to Jerusalem and to the house of Judah; do not be afraid [Zechariah 8:15].

"Fear Not" in New Testament Gospels

In the Infancy Narratives

Joseph, son of David, do not be afraid to take Mary as your wife, for the child conceived in her is from the Holy Spirit [Matthew 1:20].

When Zechariah saw him, he was terrified; and fear overwhelmed him. But the angel said to him, "Do not be afraid, Zechariah, for your prayer has been heard. Your wife Elizabeth will bear you a son, and you will name him John" [Luke 1:12–13].

The angel said to her, "Do not be afraid, Mary, for you have found favor with God" [Luke 1:30].

We, being rescued from the hands of our enemies, might serve him without fear [Luke 1:74].

Then an angel of the Lord stood before them, and the glory of the Lord shone around them, and they were terrified. But the angel said to them, "Do not be afraid; for see—I am bringing you good news of great joy for all the people" [Luke 2:9–10].

Jesus Calls the First Disciples

For he and all who were with him were amazed at the catch of fish that they had taken; and so also were James and John, sons of Zebedee, who were partners with Simon. Then Jesus said to Simon, "Do not be afraid; from now on you will be catching people" [Luke 5:9–10].

During a Storm at Sea

And he said to them, "Why are you afraid you of little faith?" Then he got up and rebuked the winds and the sea; and there was a dead calm [Matthew 8:26].

He said to them, "Why are you afraid? Have you still no faith?" [Mark 4:40]

Jesus Speaks to Jairus

But overhearing what they said, Jesus said to the leader of the synagogue, "Do not fear, only believe" [Mark 5:36].

When Jesus heard this, he replied, "Do not fear. Only believe, and she will be saved" [Luke 8:50].

Jesus Instructs His Disciples

So have no fear of them; for nothing is covered up that will not be uncovered, and nothing secret that will not become known [Matthew 10:26].

Do not fear those who kill the body but cannot kill the soul; rather fear him who can destroy both soul and body in hell [Matthew 10:28].

So do not be afraid; you are of more value than many sparrows [Matthew 10:31].

I tell you, my friends, do not fear those who kill the body, and after that can do nothing more. But I will warn you whom to fear: fear him who, after he has killed, has authority to cast into hell. Yes, I tell you, fear him! [Luke 12:4–5]

But even the hairs of your head are all counted. Do not be afraid; you are of more value than many sparrows [Luke 12:7].

Do not be afraid, little flock, for it is your Father's good pleasure to give you the kingdom [Luke 12:32].

As Jesus Walks on Water

But when the disciples saw him walking on the sea, they were terrified, saying, "It is a ghost!" And they cried out in fear. But immediately Jesus spoke to them and said, "Take heart, it is I; do not be afraid" [Matthew 14:26–27].

But when they saw him walking on the lake, they thought it was a ghost and cried out; for they all saw him and were terrified. But immediately he spoke to them and said, "Take heart, it is I; do not be afraid" [Mark 6:49–50].

But he said to them, "It is I; do not be afraid" [John 6:20].

At the Transfiguration of Jesus

When the disciples heard this, they fell to the ground and were overcome by fear. But Jesus came and touched them, saying, "Get up and do not be afraid" [Matthew 17:6–7].

At Jesus's Entry into Jerusalem

Do not be afraid, daughter of Zion. Look, your king is coming, sitting on a donkey's colt! [John 12:15]

Jesus Teaches His Disciples in Jerusalem

And you will hear of wars and rumors of wars; see that you are not alarmed; for this must take place, but the end is not yet [Matthew 24:6].

When you hear of wars and rumors of wars, do not be alarmed; this must take place, but the end is still to come [Mark 13:7].

When you hear of wars and insurrections, do not be terrified; for these things must take place first, but the end will not follow immediately [Luke 21:9].

At the Last Supper

Do not let your hearts be troubled. Believe in God, believe also in me [John 14:1].

> *Peace I leave with you; my peace I give to you. I do not give to you as the world gives. Do not let your hearts be troubled, and do not let them be afraid* (John 14:27).

On Easter Morning at the Empty Tomb

> *For fear of him the guards shook and became like dead men. But the angel said to the women, "Do not be afraid; I know that you are looking for Jesus who was crucified."* (Matthew 28:4–5).

> *So they left the tomb quickly with fear and great joy, and ran to tell his disciples....Then Jesus said to them, "Do not be afraid; go and tell my brothers to go to Galilee; there they will see me"* (Matthew 28:8, 10).

"Fear Not" in Other New Testament Texts

Acts of the Apostles

> *One night the Lord said to Paul in a vision, "Do not be afraid, but speak and do not be silent"* (Acts 18:9).

> *Do not be afraid, Paul; you must stand before the emperor; and indeed, God has granted safety to all those who are sailing with you* (Acts 27:24).

Letters Attributed to Paul

> *For you did not receive a spirit of slavery to fall back into fear, but you have received a spirit of adoption. When we cry, "Abba! Father!"* (Romans 8:15)

> *For rulers are not a terror [lit. "not a cause for fear"] to good conduct, but to bad. Do you wish to have no fear of*

the authority? Then do what is good, and you will receive its approval [Romans 13:3].

If Timothy comes, see that he has nothing to fear among you, for he is doing the work of the Lord just as I am [1 Corinthians 16:10].

And most of the brothers and sisters, having been made confident in the Lord by my imprisonment, dare to speak the word with greater boldness and without fear [Philippians 1:14].

[I will know that you] are in no way intimidated by your opponents. For them this is evidence of their destruction, but of your salvation. And this is God's doing [Philippians 1:28].

We beg you, brothers and sisters, not to be quickly shaken in mind or alarmed, either by spirit or by word or by letter, as though from us, to the effect that the day of the Lord is already here [2 Thessalonians 2:1–2].

By faith Moses was hidden by his parents for three months after his birth, because they saw that the child was beautiful; and they were not afraid of the king's edict [Hebrews 11:23].

By faith he left Egypt, unafraid of the king's anger; for he persevered as though he saw him who is invisible [Hebrews 11:27].

So we can say with confidence, "The Lord is my helper; I will not be afraid. What can anyone do to me?" [Hebrews 13:6]

Thus Sarah obeyed Abraham and called him lord. You have become her daughters as long as you do what is good and never let fears alarm you (1 Peter 3:6).

But even if you do suffer for doing what is right, you are blessed. Do not fear what they fear, and do not be intimidated (1 Peter 3:14).

There is no fear in love, but perfect love casts out fear; for fear has to do with punishment, and whoever fears has not reached perfection in love (1 John 4:18).

Book of Revelation

When I saw him, I fell at his feet as though dead. But he placed his right hand on me, saying, "Do not be afraid; I am the first and the last" (Revelation 1:17).

Do not fear what you are about to suffer. Beware, the devil is about to throw some of you into prison so that you may be tested, and for ten days you will have affliction. Be faithful until death, and I will give you the crown of life (Revelation 2:10).

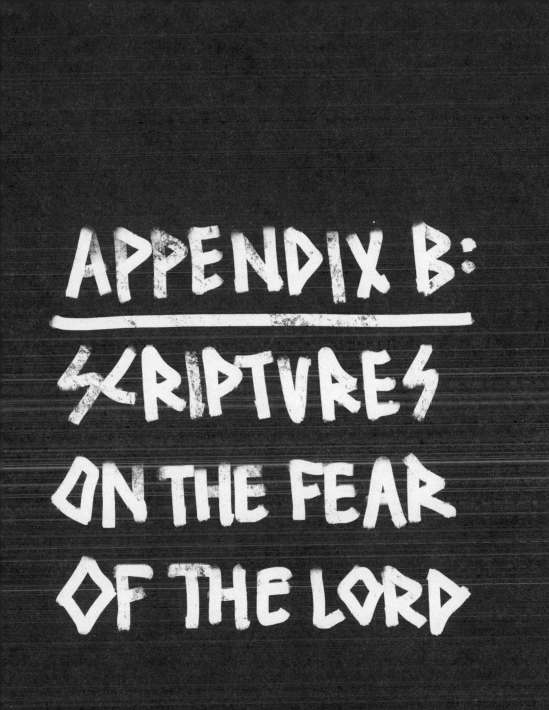

APPENDIX B:

SCRIPTURES ON THE FEAR OF THE LORD

All verses in Appendix B are from the NRSV.

OLD TESTAMENT TEXTS

Abraham said, "I did it because I thought, There is no fear of God at all in this place, and they will kill me because of my wife" [Genesis 20:11].

He said, "Do not lay your hand on the boy or do anything to him; for now I know that you fear God, since you have not withheld your son, your only son, from me" [Genesis 22:12].

On the third day Joseph said to them, "Do this and you will live, for I fear God" [Genesis 42:18].

But the midwives feared God; they did not do as the king of Egypt commanded them, but they let the boys live [Exodus 1:17].

And because the midwives feared God, he gave them families [Exodus 1:21].

Those officials of Pharaoh who feared the word of the Lord hurried their slaves and livestock off to a secure place [Exodus 9:20].

But as for you and your officials, I know that you do not yet fear the Lord God [Exodus 9:30].

Israel saw the great work that the Lord did against the Egyptians. So the people feared the Lord and believed in the Lord and in his servant Moses [Exodus 14:31].

You should also look for able men among all the people, men who fear God, are trustworthy, and hate dishonest gain; set such men over them as officers over thousands, hundreds, fifties, and tens [Exodus 18:21].

You shall not revile the deaf or put a stumbling-block before the blind; you shall fear your God: I am the Lord [Leviticus 19:14].

You shall rise before the aged, and defer to the old; and you shall fear your God: I am the Lord [Leviticus 19:32].

Do not take interest in advance or otherwise make a profit from them, but fear your God; let them live with you [Leviticus 25:36].

You shall not rule over them with harshness, but shall fear your God [Leviticus 25:43].

So that you and your children and your children's children may fear the Lord your God all the days of your life, and keep all his decrees and his commandments that I am commanding you, so that your days may be long [Deuteronomy 6:2].

Then the Lord commanded us to observe all these statutes, to fear the Lord our God, for our lasting good, so as to keep us alive, as is now the case [Deuteronomy 6:24].

Therefore keep the commandments of the Lord your God, by walking in his ways and by fearing him [Deuteronomy 8:6].

So now, O Israel, what does the Lord your God require of you? Only to fear the Lord your God, to walk in all his ways, to love him, to serve the Lord your God with all your heart and with all your soul [Deuteronomy 10:12].

You shall fear the Lord your God; him alone you shall worship; to him you shall hold fast, and by his name you shall swear (Deuteronomy 10:20).

In the presence of the Lord your God, in the place that he will choose as a dwelling for his name, you shall eat the tithe of your grain, your wine, and your oil, as well as the firstlings of your herd and flock, so that you may learn to fear the Lord your God always (Deuteronomy 14:23).

It shall remain with him and he shall read in it all the days of his life, so that he may learn to fear the Lord his God, diligently observing all the words of this law and these statutes (Deuteronomy 17:19).

How he attacked you on the way, when you were faint and weary, and struck down all who lagged behind you; he did not fear God (Deuteronomy 25:18).

Assemble the people—men, women, and children, as well as the aliens residing in your towns—so that they may hear and learn to fear the Lord your God and to observe diligently all the words of this law (Deuteronomy 31:12).

So that their children, who have not known it, may hear and learn to fear the Lord your God, as long as you live in the land that you are crossing over the Jordan to possess (Deuteronomy 31:13).

So that all the peoples of the earth may know that the hand of the Lord is mighty, and so that you may fear the Lord your God for ever (Joshua 4:24).

If you will fear the Lord and serve him and heed his voice and not rebel against the commandment of the Lord, and if both you and the king who reigns over you will follow the Lord your God, it will be well [1 Samuel 12:14].

Only fear the Lord, and serve him faithfully with all your heart; for consider what great things he has done for you [1 Samuel 12:24].

The God of Israel has spoken, the Rock of Israel has said to me: One who rules over people justly, ruling in the fear of God [2 Samuel 23:3].

Now the wife of a member of the company of prophets cried to Elisha, "Your servant my husband is dead; and you know that your servant feared the Lord, but a creditor has come to take my two children as slaves" [2 Kings 4:1].

They defeated all the cities around Gerar, for the fear of the Lord was on them. They plundered all the cities; for there was much plunder in them [2 Chronicles 14:14].

The fear of the Lord fell on all the kingdoms of the lands around Judah, and they did not make war against Jehoshaphat [2 Chronicles 17:10].

Now, let the fear of the Lord be upon you; take care what you do, for there is no perversion of justice with the Lord our God, or partiality, or taking of bribes [2 Chronicles 19:7].

He charged them: "This is how you shall act: in the fear of the Lord, in faithfulness, and with your whole heart" [2 Chronicles 19:9].

The fear of God came on all the kingdoms of the countries [2 Chronicles 20:29].

He set himself to seek God in the days of Zechariah, who instructed him in the fear of God; and as long as he sought the Lord, God made him prosper (2 Chronicles 26:5).

So I said, "The thing that you are doing is not good. Should you not walk in the fear of our God, to prevent the taunts of the nations our enemies?" (Nehemiah 5:9)

I gave my brother Hanani charge over Jerusalem, along with Hananiah the commander of the citadel—for he was a faithful man and feared God more than many (Nehemiah 7:2).

There was once a man in the land of Uz whose name was Job. That man was blameless and upright, one who feared God and turned away from evil (Job 1:1).

The Lord said to Satan, "Have you considered my servant Job? There is no one like him on the earth, a blameless and upright man who fears God and turns away from evil" (Job 1:8).

Then Satan answered the Lord, "Does Job fear God for nothing?" (Job 1:9)

The Lord said to Satan, "Have you considered my servant Job? There is no one like him on the earth, a blameless and upright man who fears God and turns away from evil. He still persists in his integrity, although you incited me against him, to destroy him for no reason" (Job 2:3).

Is not your fear of God your confidence, and the integrity of your ways your hope? (Job 4:6)

But you are doing away with the fear of God, and hindering meditation before God (Job 15:4).

Dominion and fear are with God; he makes peace in his high heaven (Job 25:2).

And he said to humankind, "Truly, the fear of the Lord, that is wisdom; and to depart from evil is understanding" (Job 28:28).

Put them in fear, O Lord; let the nations know that they are only human (Psalm 9:20).

In whose eyes the wicked are despised, but who honor those who fear the Lord; who stand by their oath even to their hurt (Psalm 15:4).

The fear of the Lord is pure, enduring for ever; the ordinances of the Lord are true and righteous altogether (Psalm 19:9).

You who fear the Lord, praise him! All you offspring of Jacob, glorify him; stand in awe of him, all you offspring of Israel! (Psalm 22:23)

Who are they that fear the Lord? He will teach them the way that they should choose (Psalm 25:12).

Let all the earth fear the Lord; let all the inhabitants of the world stand in awe of him (Psalm 33:8).

O fear the Lord, you his holy ones, for those who fear him have no want (Psalm 34:9).

Come, O children, listen to me; I will teach you the fear of the Lord (Psalm 34:11).

Transgression speaks to the wicked deep in their hearts; there is no fear of God before their eyes (Psalm 36:1).

God, who is enthroned from of old...will hear, and will humble them—because they do not change, and do not fear God (Psalm 55:19).

Come and hear, all you who fear God, and I will tell what he has done for me (Psalm 66:16).

The nations will fear the name of the Lord, and all the kings of the earth your glory (Psalm 102:15).

The fear of the Lord is the beginning of wisdom; all those who practise it have a good understanding. His praise endures forever (Psalm 111:10).

Praise the Lord! Happy are those who fear the Lord, who greatly delight in his commandments (Psalm 112:1).

You who fear the Lord, trust in the Lord! He is their help and their shield (Psalm 115:11).

He will bless those who fear the Lord, both small and great (Psalm 115:13).

Let those who fear the Lord say, "His steadfast love endures for ever" (Psalm 118:4).

Happy is everyone who fears the Lord, who walks in his ways (Psalm 128:1).

Thus shall the man be blessed who fears the Lord (Psalm 128:4).

O house of Levi, bless the Lord! You that fear the Lord, bless the Lord! (Psalm 135:20)

The fear of the Lord is the beginning of knowledge; fools despise wisdom and instruction (Proverbs 1:7).

Because they hated knowledge and did not choose the fear of the Lord (Proverbs 1:29).

Then you will understand the fear of the Lord and find the knowledge of God (Proverbs 2:5).

Do not be wise in your own eyes; fear the Lord, and turn away from evil (Proverbs 3:7).

The fear of the Lord is hatred of evil. Pride and arrogance and the way of evil and perverted speech I hate (Proverbs 8:13).

The fear of the Lord is the beginning of wisdom, and the knowledge of the Holy One is insight (Proverbs 9:10).

The fear of the Lord prolongs life, but the years of the wicked will be short (Proverbs 10:27).

Those who walk uprightly fear the Lord, but one who is devious in conduct despises him (Proverbs 14:2).

In the fear of the Lord one has strong confidence, and one's children will have a refuge (Proverbs 14:26).

The fear of the Lord is a fountain of life, so that one may avoid the snares of death (Proverbs 14:27).

Better is a little with the fear of the Lord than great treasure and trouble with it (Proverbs 15:16).

The fear of the Lord is instruction in wisdom, and humility goes before honor (Proverbs 15:33).

By loyalty and faithfulness iniquity is atoned for, and by the fear of the Lord one avoids evil (Proverbs 16:6).

The fear of the Lord is life indeed; filled with it one rests secure and suffers no harm (Proverbs 19:23).

The reward for humility and fear of the Lord is riches and honor and life (Proverbs 22:4).

Do not let your heart envy sinners, but always continue in the fear of the Lord (Proverbs 23:17).

My child, fear the Lord and the king, and do not disobey either of them (Proverbs 24:21).

Charm is deceitful, and beauty is vain, but a woman who fears the Lord is to be praised (Proverbs 31:30).

With many dreams come vanities and a multitude of words; but fear God (Ecclesiastes 5:7).

It is good that you should take hold of the one, without letting go of the other; for the one who fears God shall succeed with both (Ecclesiastes 7:18).

It will not be well with the wicked, neither will they prolong their days like a shadow, because they do not stand in fear before God (Ecclesiastes 8:13).

The end of the matter; all has been heard. Fear God, and keep his commandments; for that is the whole duty of everyone (Ecclesiastes 12:13).

Those who fear the Lord will not be timid, or play the coward, for he is their hope (Sirach 34:16).

The spirit of the Lord shall rest on him, the spirit of wisdom and understanding, the spirit of counsel and might, the spirit of knowledge and the fear of the Lord (Isaiah 11:2).

His delight shall be in the fear of the Lord. He shall not judge by what his eyes see, or decide by what his ears hear (Isaiah 11:3).

He will be the stability of your times, abundance of salvation, wisdom, and knowledge; the fear of the Lord is Zion's treasure (Isaiah 33:6).

Who among you fears the Lord and obeys the voice of his servant, who walks in darkness and has no light, yet trusts in the name of the Lord and relies upon his God? (Isaiah 50:10)

Whom did you dread and fear so that you lied, and did not remember me or give me a thought? Have I not kept silent and closed my eyes, and so you do not fear me? (Isaiah 57:11)

So those in the west shall fear the name of the Lord, and those in the east, his glory: for he will come like a pent-up stream that the wind of the Lord drives on (Isaiah 59:19).

Why, O Lord, do you make us stray from your ways and harden our heart, so that we do not fear you? Turn back for the sake of your servants, for the sake of the tribes that are your heritage (Isaiah 63:17).

Do you not fear me? says the Lord; Do you not tremble before me? I placed the sand as a boundary for the sea, a perpetual barrier that it cannot pass; though the waves toss, they cannot prevail, though they roar, they cannot pass over it (Jeremiah 5:22).

They do not say in their hearts, "Let us fear the Lord our God, who gives the rain in its season, the autumn rain and the spring rain, and keeps for us the weeks appointed for the harvest" (Jeremiah 5:24).

Who would not fear you, O King of the nations? For that is your due; among all the wise ones of the nations and in all their kingdoms there is no one like you (Jeremiah 10:7).

Did King Hezekiah of Judah and all Judah actually put him to death? Did he not fear the Lord and entreat the favor of the Lord, and did not the Lord change his mind about the disaster that he had pronounced against them? But we are about to bring great disaster on ourselves! (Jeremiah 26:19)

I make a decree, that in all my royal dominion people should tremble and fear before the God of Daniel: For he is the living God, enduring for ever. His kingdom shall never be destroyed, and his dominion has no end (Daniel 6:26).

For now they will say: "We have no king, for we do not fear the Lord, and a king—what could he do for us?" (Hosea 10:3)

Then the men feared the Lord even more, and they offered a sacrifice to the Lord and made vows (Jonah 1:16).

They shall lick dust like a snake, like the crawling things of the earth; they shall come trembling out of their fortresses; they shall turn in dread to the Lord our God, and they shall stand in fear of you (Micah 7:17).

Then Zerubbabel son of Shealtiel, and Joshua son of Jehozadak, the high priest, with all the remnant of the people, obeyed the voice of the Lord their God, and the words of the prophet Haggai, as the Lord their God had sent him; and the people feared the Lord [Haggai 1:12].

Then I will draw near to you for judgement; I will be swift to bear witness against the sorcerers, against the adulterers, against those who swear falsely, against those who oppress the hired workers in their wages, the widow, and the orphan, against those who thrust aside the alien, and do not fear me, says the Lord of hosts [Malachi 3:5].

NEW TESTAMENT TEXTS

This list includes verses that imply appropriate reverence toward God.

When the crowds saw it, they were filled with awe, and they glorified God, who had given such authority to human beings [Matthew 9:8].

And they were filled with great awe and said to one another, "Who then is this, that even the wind and the sea obey him?" [Mark 4:41]

His mercy is for those who fear him [God] from generation to generation [Luke 1:50].

Amazement seized all of them, and they glorified God and were filled with awe, saying, "We have seen strange things today." [Luke 5:26].

He said, "In a certain city there was a judge who neither feared God nor had respect for people" [Luke 18:2].

For a while he refused; but later he said to himself, "Though I have no fear of God and no respect for anyone" [Luke 18:4].

But the other rebuked him, saying, "Do you not fear God, since you are under the same sentence of condemnation?" [Luke 23:40]

Awe came upon everyone, because many wonders and signs were being done by the apostles [Acts 2:43].

Meanwhile the church throughout Judea, Galilee, and Samaria had peace and was built up. Living in the fear of the Lord and in the comfort of the Holy Spirit, it increased in numbers [Acts 9:31].

He was a devout man who feared God with all his household; he gave alms generously to the people and prayed constantly to God [Acts 10:2].

They answered, "Cornelius, a centurion, an upright and God-fearing man, who is well spoken of by the whole Jewish nation, was directed by a holy angel to send for you to come to his house and to hear what you have to say" [Acts 10:22].

In every nation anyone who fears him and does what is right is acceptable to him [Acts 10:35].

So Paul stood up and with a gesture began to speak: "You Israelites, and others who fear God, listen" [Acts 13:16].

My brothers, you descendants of Abraham's family, and others who fear God, to us the message of this salvation has been sent (Acts 13:26).

When this became known to all residents of Ephesus, both Jews and Greeks, everyone was awestruck; and the name of the Lord Jesus was praised (Acts 19:17).

There is no fear of God before their eyes (Romans 3:18).

That is true. They were broken off because of their unbelief, but you stand only through faith. So do not become proud, but stand in awe (Romans 11:20).

Therefore, knowing the fear of the Lord, we try to persuade others; but we ourselves are well known to God, and I hope that we are also well known to your consciences (2 Corinthians 5:11).

Since we have these promises, beloved, let us cleanse ourselves from every defilement of body and of spirit, making holiness perfect in the fear of God (2 Corinthians 7:1).

And his heart goes out all the more to you, as he remembers the obedience of all of you, and how you welcomed him with fear and trembling (2 Corinthians 7:15).

Be subject to one another out of reverence for Christ (Ephesians 5:21).

Each of you, however, should love his wife as himself, and a wife should respect [lit. "fear"] her husband (Ephesians 5:33).

Slaves, obey your earthly masters with fear and trembling, in singleness of heart, as you obey Christ (Ephesians 6:5).

Therefore, my beloved, just as you have always obeyed me, not only in my presence, but much more now in my absence, work out your own salvation with fear and trembling (Philippians 2:12).

Slaves, obey your earthly masters in everything, not only while being watched and in order to please them, but wholeheartedly, fearing the Lord (Colossians 3:22).

Therefore, while the promise of entering his rest is still open, let us take care that none of you should seem to have failed to reach it (Hebrews 4:1).

It is a fearful thing to fall into the hands of the living God (Hebrews 10:31).

Indeed, so terrifying was the sight that Moses said, "I tremble with fear" (Hebrews 12:21).

If you invoke as Father the one who judges all people impartially according to their deeds, live in reverent fear during the time of your exile (1 Peter 1:17).

Honor everyone. Love the family of believers. Fear God. Honor the emperor. Slaves, accept the authority of your masters with all deference, not only those who are kind and gentle but also those who are harsh (1 Peter 2:17–18).

[Non-believing husbands may be won over by their wives' conduct] when they see the purity and reverence of your lives (1 Peter 3:1–2).

Always be ready to make your defence...yet do it with gentleness and reverence. Keep your conscience clear, so that, when you are maligned, those who abuse you for your good conduct in Christ may be put to shame (1 Peter 3:15–16).

The nations raged, but your wrath has come, and the time for judging the dead, for rewarding your servants, the prophets and saints and all who fear your name, both small and great, and for destroying those who destroy the earth (Revelation 11:18).

He said in a loud voice, "Fear God and give him glory, for the hour of his judgement has come; and worship him who made heaven and earth, the sea and the springs of water" (Revelation 14:7).

Lord, who will not fear and glorify your name? For you alone are holy. All nations will come and worship before you, for your judgements have been revealed (Revelation 15:4).

And from the throne came a voice saying, "Praise our God, all you his servants, and all who fear him, small and great" (Revelation 19:5).

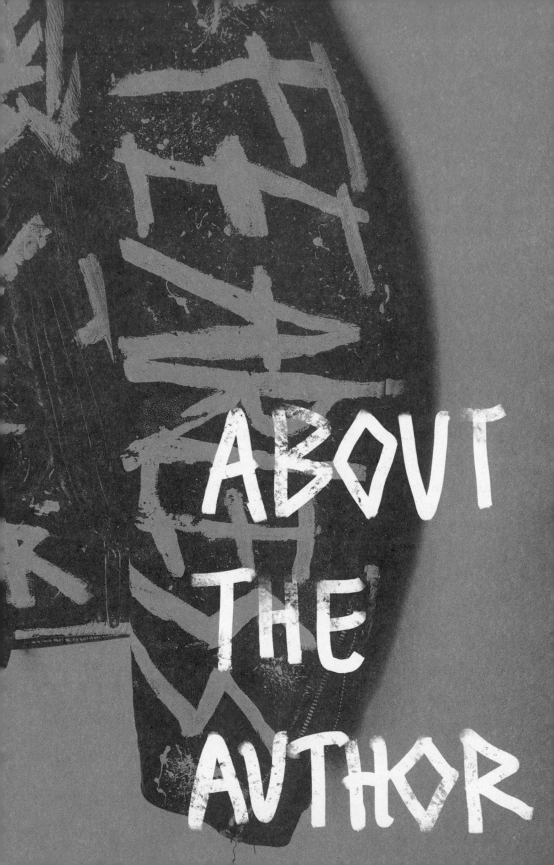

ABOUT THE AUTHOR

Jeremy Johnson leads Fearless Church and Love More with his wife, Christy, and their three children, Lyric, Brave, and Arrow. Located in the heart of downtown Los Angeles, Orange County, and San Diego they and their team have a call to serve their cities and the state of California to make an impact worldwide through the life-transforming message of Jesus's power and love. In 2006 the couple founded the Worth Dying For band and the Ammunition Conference, which is attended by thousands of young adults and senior leaders hungry for a move of God. It was out of this conference that Fearless Church, Fearless Conference, and Fearless BND were born. Widely known for his creativity and fearless passion, Jeremy travels internationally with a fearless message to see revival spark in his generation and transform culture. He has committed his life to seeing the dreamers rise and fulfill their God-given purpose. Experiencing freedom from fear in his personal life, he longs to see others live fearlessly through the perfect love of Christ. The Fearless ministry is built upon this creed formed from 1 John 4:18, which states, *"There is no fear in love. But perfect love drives out fear."*

If you would like to follow Jeremy and Fearless

@jeremyjohnsonla

@fearless_la

FEARLESS

The mission of Fearless church is to Love More and Fear Less. With the original campus beginning in the heart of downtown Los Angeles nine years ago, they have since started three additional campuses in Orange County, San Diego, and online reaching thousands of people weekly all over the globe. They activate their mission through their weekly outreach initiatives at all campuses, distributing food and resources to those in need. In the last two years, they have been able to bless families with a total number of 4,297,000 pounds of groceries! They plan to expand their efforts, ensuring that their communities do not go hungry and experience the love of Jesus through their ministry.

www.fearless.church

For more information about the Fearless movement and additional elements created in partnership with this book by Jeremy Johnson, visit: www.declarewaronfear.com or scan the QR code below.